World Link | Developing English Fluency

Susan Stempleski
Nancy Douglas • James R. Morgan

THOMSON

HEINLE

Australia · Canada · Mexico · Singapore · Spain · United Kingdom · United States

World Link 2, Student Book

Susan Stempleski

Nancy Douglas • *James R. Morgan*

Publisher: Christopher Wenger
Director of Marketing: Amy Mabley
Director of Product Development: Anita Raducanu
Acquisitions Editor: Mary Sutton-Paul
Sr. Marketing Manager: Eric Bredenberg
Developmental Editor: Paul MacIntyre
Production Manager: Sally Cogliano
Sr. Print Buyer: Mary Beth Hennebury

Compositor: Christopher Hanzie, Ronn Lee, TYA Inc.
Project Manager: Christopher Hanzie
Photography Manager: Sheri Blaney
Photo Researcher: Christopher Hanzie, Ronn Lee
Illustrator: Raketshop Design Studio (Philippines),
   Melvin Chong (Singapore)
Cover/Text Designer: Christopher Hanzie, TYA Inc.
Printer: Transcontinental Printing
Cover Image: TYA Inc. PhotoDisc, Inc.

Printed in Canada.
1 2 3 4 5 6 7 8 9 10   08 07 06 05 04

For more information contact Thomson Heinle
25 Thomson Place, Boston, MA 02210 USA, or you
can visit our Internet site at http://www.thomson.com

For permission to use material from this text or product, submit a request online at http://www.thomsonrights.com Any additional questions about permissions can be submitted by email to thomsonrights@thomson.com

ISBN: 0-8384-0665-3
Library of Congress Number: 2004107174

Photo Credits

Unless otherwise stated, all photos are from PhotoDisc, Inc. Digital Imagery © copyright 2005 PhotoDisc, Inc. and TYA Inc. Photos from other sources: page 12 : (chili) Great American Stock/Index Stock Imagery; page 19: Reuters/CORBIS; page 20 : (bottom) David Turnley/CORBIS; page 23: Bettmen/CORBIS; page 25: Gianni Dagli Orti/CORBIS; page 26: Bettman/CORBIS; page 31: (top left) ImageState Royalty Free/Alamy, (top right) Ron Russell/Index Stock Imagery, (bottom left) Bettmen/CORBIS, (bottom right) Bettman/CORBIS; page 42 (center): Brand X Pictures/Alamy; page 51 (left): Brand X Pictures/Alamy; page 52: ImageState/Alamy; page 57: John Heseltine/CORBIS; page 65 (Prince William): (top) Graham Tim/ CORBIS SYGMA, (bottom) Reuters/CORBIS; page 75: (left) Kenneth Hamm/Photo Japan, (right) Lindsay Hebberd/CORBIS; page 76: Richard Powers/CORBIS; page 77: Reuters/CORBIS; page 79: Setboun/CORBIS; page 82: Dreamworks LCC/THE KOBAL COLLECTION; page 83: Walt Disney Company; page 87: Walt Disney Storyline/Citadel/THE KOBAL COLLECTION; page 90: PHOTOTAKE Inc./ALAMY; page 91: THE KOBAL COLLECTION; page 95: (top row left) Layne Kennedy/CORBIS, (top row second left) Michael Arnaud/CORBIS; page 96: Layne Kennedy/CORBIS; page 99: Joe Sohm/Alamy, Paul A. Souders/ COBRBIS, Rob Rowan/Progressive Photos/CORBIS, Vittoriano Rastelli/CORBIS, Owen Franklin/CORBIS; page 102: (far left)Hemera Photo Objects, (far right)Dean Conger/CORBIS; page 115: Judith Collins/Alamy; page 118 (top): Kenneth Hamm/Photo Japan; page 121: Reuters/CORBIS; page 122: (left) Roger Ressmeyer/CORBIS, (center) John D. Luke/Index Stock Imagery, (right) Alain Nogues/CORBIS; page 123: (top left) SHANKEN DANIEL/CORBIS SYGMA, (top righth) Reuters/CORBIS, (bottom left) JOHN HILLARY/Reauters/Corbis; page 128: (sleeping bag, Swiss army knife) Hemera Photo Objects, (chewing gum) Peter Ardito/INDEX STOCK PHOTO; page 132: Ken Welsh/Alamy

Every effort has been made to trace all sources of illustrations/photos/information in this book, but if any have been inadvertently overlooked, the publisher will be pleased to make the necessary arrangements at the first opportunity.

Acknowledgments

We would firstly like to thank the educators who provided invaluable feedback throughout the development of the *World Link* series:

Byung-kyoo Ahn, Chonnam National University; Elisabeth Blom, Casa Thomas Jefferson; Grazyna Anna Bonomi; Vera Burlamaqui Bradford, Instituto Brasil-Estados Unidos; Araceli Cabanillas Carrasco, Universidad Autónoma de Sinaloa; Silvania Capua Carvalho, State University of Feira de Santana; Tânia Branco Cavaignac, Casa Branca Idiomas; Kyung-whan Cha, Chung-Ang University; Chwun-li Chen, Shih Chien University; María Teresa Fátima Encinas, Universidad Iberoamericana-Puebla and Universidad Autónoma de Puebla; Sandra Gaviria, Universidad EAFIT; Marina González, Instituto de Lenguas Modernas; Frank Graziani, Tokai University; Chi-ying Fione Huang, Ming Chuan University; Shu-fen Huang (Jessie), Chung Hua University; Tsai, Shwu Hui (Ellen), Chung Kuo Institute of Technology and Commerce; Connie R. Johnson, Universidad de las Américas-Puebla; Diana Jones, Instituto Angloamericano; Annette Kaye, Kyoritsu Women's University; Lee, Kil-ryoung, Yeungnam University; David Kluge, Kinjo Gakuin University; Nancy H. Lake; Hyunoo Lee, Inha University; Amy Peijung Lee, Hsuan Chuang College; Hsiu-Yun Liao, Chinese Culture University; Yuh-Huey Gladys Lin, Chung Hua University; Eleanor Occeña, Universitaria de Idiomas, Universidad Autónoma del Estado de Hidalgo; Laura Pérez Palacio, Tecnológico de Monterrey; Doraci Perez Mak, União Cultural Brasil-Estados Unidos; Mae-Ran Park, Pukyong National University; Joo-Kyung Park, Honam University; Bill Pellowe, Kinki University; Margareth Perucci, Sociedade Brasileira de Cultura Inglesa; Nevitt Reagan, Kansai Gaidai University; Lesley D. Riley, Kanazawa Institute of Technology; Ramiro Luna Rivera, Tecnológico de Monterrey, Prepa; Marie Adele Ryan, Associação Alumni; Michael Shawback, Ritsumeikan University; Kathryn Singh, ITESM; Grant Trew, Nova Group; Michael Wu, Chung Hua University

---

A great many people participated in the making of the *World Link* series. In particular I would like to thank the authors, Nancy Douglas and James Morgan, for all their hard work, creativity, and good humor. I would also like to give special thanks to the developmental editor Paul MacIntyre, whose good judgment and careful attention to detail were invaluable. Thanks, too, to publisher Chris Wenger, and all the other wonderful people at Thomson/Heinle who have worked on this project. I am also very grateful to the many reviewers around the world, whose insightful comments on early drafts of the *World Link* materials were much appreciated.
Susan Stempleski

We'd like to extend a very special thank you to two individuals at Thomson/Heinle: Chris Wenger for spearheading the project and providing leadership, support and guidance throughout the development of the series, and Paul MacIntyre for his detailed and insightful editing, and his tireless commitment to this project. We also offer our sincere thanks to Susan Stempleski, whose extensive experience and invaluable feedback helped to the shape the material in this book.

Thanks also go to those on the editorial, production, and support teams who helped to make this book happen: Anita Raducanu, Sally Cogliano, David Bohlke, Christine Galvin-Combet, Lisa Geraghty, Carmen Corral-Reid, Jean Pender, Rebecca Klevberg, Mary Sutton-Paul, and their colleagues in Asia and Latin America.

I would also like to thank my parents, Alexander and Patricia, for their love and encouragement. And to my husband Jorge and daughter Jasmine—thank you for your patience and faith in me. I couldn't have done this without you!
Nancy Douglas

I would also like to thank my mother, Frances P. Morgan, for her unflagging support and my father, Lee Morgan Jr., for instilling the love of language and learning in me.
James R. Morgan

World Link Level 2   *Scope and Sequence*

Reading & Writing	Language Link	Communication
		Unit 1
"A book of memories": Reading about high school yearbooks	The simple present vs. the present continuous	"Is it you?": Guessing classmates' identities by their habits
"Signing a yearbook": Writing a yearbook-style graduation message	Review of the simple past	"Class awards": Selecting classmates to receive various awards
		Unit 2
"The healthiest people in the world". Reading about the longevity of Okinawans	The comparative form of adjectives	"Veronica's Restaurant": Creating a radio advertisement for a new and improved restaurant
"Restaurant review": Writing a restaurant review	The superlative form of adjectives	"Comparing foods": Creating a menu for a new restaurant
		Unit 3
"The Marfa mystery lights": Reading about a strange phenomenon	Stative verbs	"The Lindbergh kidnapping": Deducing the identity of the kidnapper from circumstantial evidence.
"A strange event": Writing about a mystery or strange event	Adverbs of manner	"It's a big hoax": Comparing opinions about mysteries and hoaxes

Reading & Writing	Language Link	Communication
		Unit 4
"Trendspotting": Reading about an unusual job	Quantity expressions	"Modern opinions": Surveying classmates' opinions about life and work
"You should get a makeover": Writing a letter requesting advice on style	Giving advice with *could*, *should*, *ought to*, and *had better*	"Do you need a makeover?": Using a survey to gauge your partner's trendiness
		Unit 5
"Surprising neighborhoods": Reading about two special neighborhoods	Polite requests with modal verbs and *mind*	"An errand service": Role-playing a conversation with an errand serivce
"Come to my neighborhood.": Writing about your neighborhood	Imperatives	"Do this!": Making and performing conversations about pictured scenarios
		Unit 6
"How I plan to spend my summer vacation": Reading about a fun summer job	Plans and decisions with *be going to* and *will*	"A day on campus": Creating schedules and negotiating a time to meet
"My life now and in the future": Writing predictions about your future	Predictions with *be going to* and *will*	"Predicting the future": Using a personal profile to make predictions about your partner's future

Reading & Writing	Language Link	Communication

All About Me

Lesson A | The people in my life

1 Vocabulary Link

Talking about relationships

A Read about these people in Mario's life. Then match each of Mario's statements (1-6) below with a person. Use each statement only once.

Mr. Otani is Mario's supervisor.

Mandy is an acquaintance of Mario's.

Jada is Mario's colleague.

Jan and Mario are dating.

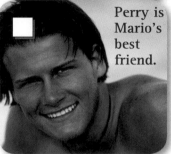

Perry is Mario's best friend.

Teresa is related to Mario.

1. "He is the boss in my office."
2. "He's a great guy. We like doing things together."
3. "She's my girlfriend."
4. "She's my cousin."
5. "We met once—at a party."
6. "We work in the same office every day."

B Pair work. Who would you talk to in the situations below? Choose from the words in the box or use your own ideas. Explain your answers to a partner.

> acquaintance   colleague   parent   best friend   girlfriend/boyfriend   supervisor

1. You break up with your boyfriend/girlfriend.
2. You have problems with a colleague.
3. You have some exciting news.
4. You have a secret to tell.

C Pair work. Make a list of people you know. Then exchange lists with a partner. Interview each other about the people on the list. Tell your partner two facts about each person.

So, who is Lucy?

She's my best friend. We met ten years ago!

2 Listening

Nosy Nora

 A Katherine is moving into an apartment. She is meeting Nora for the first time. Listen to the conversation. What do you think *nosy* means? (CD 1, Track 1)

 B Listen again. What do you know about the people in each apartment? Check (✓) all the answers that apply. (CD 1, Track 2)

1. Nora Nelson	2. Wes and Lydia	3. Two boys	4. Mrs. Hanson
✓ She's nosy.	☐ They're quiet.	☐ They're classmates.	☐ She's related to Nora.
☐ She lives in 2A.	☐ They live in 3B.	☐ They live in 2B.	☐ She lives in 3C.

ask & ANSWER

What are some people nosy about?
Do you know any nosy people?

World Link

The average U.S. citizen moves thirteen times in his or her lifetime.

3 Pronunciation

Reduction of present continuous -*ing* ending

 A Pair work. Listen to the conversations. Notice how the underlined verbs are pronounced. Then practice with a partner. (CD 1, Track 3)

Conversation 1	Conversation 2
Sandy: Hello?	Josh: Hello?
Joe: Hi, Sandy. It's Joe.	Lisa: Hi, Josh, how are you?
Sandy: Oh hi, Joe.	Josh: I'm really busy.
Joe: What are you <u>doing</u>?	Lisa: Why? What are you <u>doing</u>?
Sandy: I'm <u>sleeping</u>.	Josh: I'm <u>painting</u> my bedroom.
Joe: Oh, sorry.	Lisa: O.K. Talk to you later!

B Pair work. Practice reading the sentences below with a partner. Use the reduced pronunciation of –*ing*.

1. He's dating a really nice girl.
2. I'm fixing my car.
3. She's working in her garden.
4. We're going to the movies.

 C Now listen and check your pronunciation. (CD 1, Track 4)

4 Speaking

I'd like you to meet . . .

 A Listen to the conversations.
Who is meeting for the first time? (CD 1, Track 5)

Conversation 1

Maria:	Hi, Junko.
Junko:	Hi, Maria. It's good to see you again! How are you?
Maria:	I'm fine, thanks. How about you?
Junko:	I'm fine.
Maria:	Junko, this is Ricardo. We're classmates. We're both taking accounting this semester.
Junko:	Hi, Ricardo.
Ricardo:	Hi, Junko.

Conversation 2

Yong Il:	Hi. Let me introduce myself. I'm Yong Il.
Ileana:	Nice to meet you. My name is Ileana.
Yong Il:	It's nice to meet you, too, Ileana. I'd like you to meet Tammy.
Ileana:	Nice to meet you, Tammy.
Tammy:	Nice to meet you, too, Ileana.
Yong Il:	We're colleagues. We work in the same department.

 B Group work. Practice Conversation 1 with a partner.
Then practice Conversation 2 with two partners.

ask**&**
ANSWER

What does Maria say to introduce Ricardo?
What does Yong Il say to introduce Tammy?

5 Speaking Strategy

Introducing someone to someone else

 A Group work. Role play.
Work in groups of three: Student A, Student B, and Student C.

1. Student A: Choose a famous person to be. Write down your identity on a piece of paper and give it to Student B.

2. Student B: Read the identity of Student A. Then introduce Student A to Student C.

3. Change roles and follow steps 1 and 2 again.

> **Useful Expressions:**
> Informal introductions
>
> Junko, this is Ricardo.
> Junko, meet Ricardo.
>
> Formal introductions
>
> I'd like you to meet Tammy.
> Let me introduce Tammy.

 B Class activity. Role play.
Now introduce the "famous friends" you met in A to your other classmates. Use formal or informal style.

Ana, I'd like you to meet Enrique Iglesias.

It's nice to meet you, Enrique. My name is Ana.

It's nice to meet you too, Ana.

6 Language Link

The simple present vs. the present co...

A Look at the pictures and read a
Then use the words in the box ...ences.

right now   routine   temporary

Diane works in the sales department. She always arrives at work at 8:00 a.m.

Diane is talking on the telephone. She is also typing a report.

People are sick in the finance department. Diane is working in that department this week only.

1. This is a habit or _____. Use the simple present.

2. These events are happening _____. Use the present continuous.

3. This is a _____ situation. Use the present continuous.

B Complete these sentences to make questions in the simple present or the present continuous. Use the verbs in the box.

do   eat   have   read   sleep   ~~work~~

> You can also use the simple present for general facts.
> *My family lives in Mexico.*

1. A: You're not in the office. Where _are you working_?
   B: At home. It's only for one week.

2. A: What _____ ?
   B: A book. It's really good.

3. A: When _____ breakfast?
   B: About 7:00, usually.

4. A: How many brothers and sisters _____?
   B: Four brothers and one sister.

5. A: What _____ on the weekends?
   B: Play golf. And relax.

6. A: Who _____ in the bedroom?
   B: It's Joe. Please be very quiet.

C Véronique Lesarg is a doctor. Use the simple present or present continuous to complete her profile.

> The verb *be* is not usually used in the present continuous.

My name ____is____ (be) Véronique Lesarg. I _____ (live) in Montreal. I _____ (be) a pediatrician, a doctor for children. I usually _____ (work) in a hospital, but at the moment, I _____ (volunteer) for an organization called Doctors Without Borders. They _____ (send) staff to other countries. Right now, I _____ (work) in Africa. We _____ (build) a new clinic.

7 Communication

Is it you?

A On a sheet of paper, start a list using the simple present. Write down the following:

1. a routine you never change
2. an unusual habit
3. a general fact about yourself

Continue your list using the present continuous. Write down the following:

4. an activity you are doing right now
5. a temporary activity you are doing
6. a project you are doing outside of class

1. I always get up at 5 a.m.
2. I sometimes eat peanut butter and tomato sandwiches.
3. I have a twin brother.
4. I'm talking to my classmates.
5. I'm taking an art class this semester.
6. I'm making a photo album.

B Fold your paper and give it to your teacher. Your teacher will mix up the papers and give you a classmate's paper.

C Class activity. Talk to your classmates. Ask questions to find out who wrote the list.

Do you always get up at 5:00 in the morning?

No! That's too early for me!

All About Me

Lesson B | My memories

1 Vocabulary Link

A record of your life

A Pair work. Are these objects related to school, work, or the government? Match each object to a place. Explain your answers to a partner. (For some objects, more than one answer is possible.)

1. ~~student ID card~~
2. diploma
3. driver's license
4. electronic organizer
5. passport
6. report card
7. resume
8. birth certificate
9. yearbook

A. School

1, _____

B. Work

_____

C. Government

_____

B Pair work. Do you have any of the objects in A at home? What memories do they hold for you? Tell your partner.

> I have a passport. Last year, I used it when I went to Vancouver.

2 Listening 🎧

Just a few old keepsakes

  A Listen to a grandmother and her grandson talking. Then number the objects from 1 to 3 in the order they are mentioned. (CD 1, Track 6)

☐ passport   ☐ diary   ☐ yearbook

  B Listen again. Complete the sentences. (CD 1, Track 7)

1. The grandmother wrote about her first keepsake / boyfriend / trip in her diary.
2. She traveled to school / America / Europe by ship / car / plane.
3. She graduated in the fifties / sixties / seventies.

 C Listen again and check your answers. (CD 1, Track 8)

ask **&**
ANSWER
Are you nostalgic (sentimental about the past)?
What keepsakes do you have? How are they special?

3 Reading 📖

A book of memories

A Pair work. Discuss these questions with a partner.

1. What memories of high school do you have?
2. What clubs or activities did you join?
3. What was your favorite subject?

World Link

Making memories:
Americans take 17 billion
photos per year.

Source: *Photo Techniques,*
by Jerry O'Neil

B Read the article.

Yearbooks in the United States

Most high schools in the United States publish a yearbook. The yearbook comes out once a year, usually in the spring. It is a record of the school year—a "book of memories" for the students.

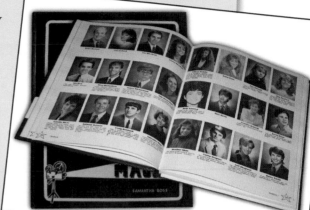

Inside a yearbook is each student's photo. The seniors are graduating soon, and their photos appear first. Next are the juniors. They are one year behind the seniors. Next come the sophomores, or second-year students. The last photos are the first-year students, the freshmen. The yearbook is not only about students. The teachers have photos, too.

The yearbook also has photos and descriptions of sports teams, academic subjects, and extracurricular activities. These are activities students do after school, such as the chess club and Spanish club. There is even a yearbook club. Students in this club write, design, and take photos all year for the yearbook. At the end of the year, the book is printed.

In the yearbook, some students receive special titles. The seniors vote and choose the "class clown" (a funny student), the "most likely to succeed" (a student everyone thinks will be successful), and the "best dressed" (a student with a good fashion sense). There are also other awards and categories.

Students typically sign each other's yearbooks. This is especially important for the seniors, because they are graduating. Students write notes to each other, such as, "We had a lot of fun," or "I'll never forget you." They also write about all the fun and funny experiences they shared in school together.

C Complete the following summary using words from the article in B.

A yearbook is a (1) __record__ of the school year. You will find each student's (2) _____ in a yearbook. Photos of the (3) _____ come first. The yearbook features (4) _____ teams, academic subjects, and extracurricular activities. There are many clubs: the (5) _____ club makes the yearbook. Seniors vote and give some students (6) _____ such as "class clown." Students (7) _____ their classmates' yearbooks. The yearbook is truly a book of (8) _____.

ask **&**
ANSWER
Did/Does your high school have a yearbook? If so, what is it like?
What sports or extracurricular activities are/were in your high school?

4 Language Link

Review of the simple past

A Edwin and Patty are looking at pictures from their high school yearbook. Read their comments.

> My freshman year was hard. I was an outsider. I didn't have a lot of friends. I often ate lunch alone. As a senior, my school life changed. I worked as the yearbook editor. I met many people and made a lot of friends.

> I was a cheerleader. We had practice every day after school. It was a lot of fun. I was also on the soccer team. We played ten games and won eight. We finished the season in first place.

B Circle the verbs in A that are in the simple past. Then write them in the chart.

Regular	*changed,*
Irregular	*was,*

C Look at these yearbook photos of three famous people. Read about them and use the simple past of the verbs to complete their histories. Then fill in their names.

	The famous "Cs"
	~~die~~ give go sing study Her mother __died__ when she was six years old. In high school, she _____ drama and dance. She _____ to New York in 1977. She _____ a song called "Vogue." She _____ concerts around the world. **Her name is:** M_____ Louise Ciccone.
	be move get play star He and his family often _____ to different places when he was young. He _____ sports in high school. He _____ bad grades. His first big movie _____ in 1983: *Risky Business.* He _____ in *The Last Samurai.* **His name is:** T_____ C_____
	die marry meet run study win When he was three months old, his father _____. He _____ hard in high school. He _____ John F. Kennedy when he was 16. He _____ his law school classmate, Hillary. He _____ for president of the United States. He _____. **His name is:** B_____ C_____

5 Writing

Signing a yearbook

A Imagine you are a senior in high school. On a separate piece of paper, write a yearbook message to a friend. Include your memories from school.

B Pair work. Exchange papers with a partner. Tell the class about one of your partner's high school memories.

Hi, Enzo. Well, we are graduating soon. We had a lot of fun over the years, didn't we? I have many good memories. Remember when we sat next to each other in math class last year? It was so boring! ...

6 Communication

Class awards

A Group work. Look at the awards below. As a group, invent one more award and write it on the ribbon.

1. Name: _____

2. Name: _____

3. Name: _____

4. Name: _____

5. Name: _____

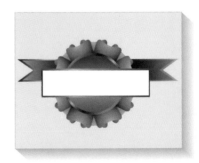

6. Name: _____

B Group work. Talk with your group about who would be the best person in your class to receive each award. Write the names under the awards.

C Group work. One person from your group tells the class your choices and the reasons.

We chose Carlos as the "friendliest." On the first day of class, he said "hello" to everyone. He also helped ...

 Check out the World Link video.

 Practice your English online at <u>worldlink.heinle.com</u>.

UNIT 2 Let's Eat!

Lesson A | Foods we like

1 Vocabulary Link

Talking about foods

A Use the adjectives in the box to talk about the foods in the pictures. Add one more adjective to the list.

The potato chips are salty and crispy. The pickles are . . .

1. buttery   7. crispy
2. crunchy   8. oily
3. sweet   9. spicy
4. bland   10. juicy
5. healthy   11. sour
6. salty   12. _____

B Describe other foods you like using the adjectives from the box.

2 Listening

Foods of the southern United States

 A Listen to Bill and Marta's conversation.
Which food *doesn't* **Marta like? Check (✓) the box.** (CD 1, Track 9)

☐ fried chicken ☐ grits ☐ fried green tomatoes ☐ Mississippi mud pie

 B **Listen again. Write the word or words Marta uses to describe each food.** (CD 1, Track 10)

1. fried chicken _____

2. grits _____

3. fried green tomatoes _____

4. Mississippi mud pie _____

ask**&**
ANSWER

Is your hometown famous for any special food?
If not, do you know a town that is famous for a special food? Describe it.

3 Pronunciation

Sentence stress and rhythm

 A **Listen and repeat the sentences. Note where the stress falls.** (CD 1, Track 11)

Oranges are sweeter than grapefruit.   Potato chips are saltier than crackers.

B **Circle the stressed syllables in these sentences.**

1. Math is harder than English.   3. The curry is spicier than the chili.

2. Apples are juicier than carrots.   4. August is hotter than July.

 C **Pair work. Listen and check your answers.**
Then practice saying the sentences with your partner.
(CD 1, Track 12)

4 Speaking

Pizza again?

 A **Listen to the conversation. Then listen again and underline the words used for suggesting.** (CD 1, Track 13)

Jill: Where do you want to go for dinner?

José: I don't know. Why don't we go to the pizza place on the corner?

Jill: Pizza again? I don't like their pizza. It's too spicy.

José: You're right. It's spicier than the pizza at Pizza House.

Jill: Well, I still want to go out tonight. How about that new Japanese restaurant downtown?

José: OK! Let's go!

B   **Pair work. Practice the conversation with a partner.**

5 Speaking Strategy

Offering and suggesting

A   **Study the Useful Expressions. Then complete the sentences below with** *Why don't we* **or** *How about*.

Useful Expressions: Offering and suggesting
You can use *Why don't we . . . ?* or *How about . . . ?* to make suggestions. *Why don't we* is followed by the base form of the verb: *Why don't we go* to the pizza place on the corner? *How about* is followed by a noun or by a verb + *ing*:   *How about the restaurant* downtown?   *How about having* a picnic in the park?

1. Can I offer you anything to eat? <u>How about</u> _____ a piece of pie?

2. _____ stop at that café? They have delicious coffee cake!

3. This museum is interesting, but I'm tired. _____ go home?

4. What time do you want to meet? _____ seven o'clock?

5. Let's go somewhere. _____ going to the beach?

6. _____ go to a movie? There's one with Jet Li that I'd love to see.

B   **Group work. Practice inviting your group's members to your favorite restaurant. They can either accept or refuse. If they refuse, they should say why.**

Why don't we go to Parr's Steakhouse for dinner?

That's a great idea!

I'm sorry, I don't eat meat. How about Indian food?

6 Language Link

The comparative form of adjectives

A Read the advertisement. Underline all the adjectives.

The comparative is often followed by *than* when comparing two things.

ANNOUNCING . . .
GRAND REOPENING!!

JOE'S CHICKEN SHACK

Yes, we are open again! Come and see the improvements:
The portions were large . . . but now they are **LARGER**!
The seating area was spacious . . . but now it is **MORE SPACIOUS**!
Our famous spicy chicken is even **SPICIER**!
Our food was good, but now it's **BETTER** than ever!

B Read the advertisement. There are two different forms of adjectives highlighted in the advertisement. How are they different?

World Link

A popular dessert in Guatemala is hot bananas served with a rich chili-flavored chocolate sauce!

C Look at the chart and fill in the missing words. Then check your answers with a partner.

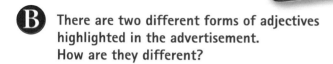

The comparative form of adjectives					
One syllable		**Two syllables**		**Three or more syllables**	
<u>sweet</u>	sweeter	_____	<u>simpler</u>	_____	more relaxing
large	_____	spicy	_____	delicious	_____
big	bigger	_____	more crowded	interesting	_____

D Complete the sentences with the comparative form of the adjective in parentheses.

1. The red curry is ____<u>spicier</u>____ than the green curry. (spicy)
2. Cherry candy is _____ than real cherries. (sweet)
3. Wow! This apple pie is _____ than my Mom's! (delicious)
4. Our English teacher is _____ than our math teacher. (nice)
5. This market is _____ on Sunday than on Monday. (crowded)
6. She is really embarrassed. Her face is _____ than an apple! (red)

E Think of foods to compare using these adjectives. Then say sentences comparing the foods.

Apples are healthier than potato chips.

good	healthy	refreshing	sweet	crispy	salty

 ask & ANSWER

Which do you like better, really spicy foods or not so spicy foods? Why?
Do you prefer foreign foods or foods from your country? Why?
Talk about drinks. Which are more refreshing? sweeter? more delicious?

Lesson A • Foods we like **15**

Veronica's Restaurant

 A Look at the pictures of Veronica's Restaurant. Talk about the changes you see. Use the adjectives in the box to help you.

clean	new	happy
bright	big	cheerful
messy	old	dirty
good	bad	nice
beautiful		

The old Veronica's

The old Veronica's is dirty.
The new Veronica's is cleaner.

The new Veronica's

 B Make notes for a radio advertisement for the new Veronica's. Include the changes you noticed in A.

_____

_____

_____

_____

_____

C Present your radio advertisement to the class.

Come and see the new Veronica's!
It's bigger and better than ever! . . .

Let's Eat!

1 Vocabulary Link

Restaurant experiences

 A Read what Sylvia and Hiro said about eating out recently. Then match the words and the definitions below.

Sylvia: I wanted to get a hamburger at the **drive-through window**, but it was closed. I parked my car and walked to a pizza place instead. I didn't want to eat in the restaurant, so I got **takeout**. Some people think that pizza is **junk food**. They say it isn't very healthy.

Hiro: I arrived at the restaurant early. I had salad for my **appetizer**, fried chicken for my **entree**, and a piece of pie for **dessert**. I couldn't eat everything, so I had to get a **doggie bag**.

__g__ 1. drive-through window   **a.** a bag or box to carry extra food home from a restaurant

_____ 2. takeout   **b.** a dish served as a main meal

_____ 3. junk food   **c.** unhealthy food

_____ 4. appetizer   **d.** a sweet food served after a meal

_____ 5. entree   **e.** food that you buy at a restaurant to eat at home

_____ 6. dessert   **f.** food eaten before the main meal

_____ 7. doggie bag   **g.** a restaurant window that serves food to people in their cars

 B Pair work. Discuss these questions with a partner.

1. What are some popular appetizers and desserts?
2. Do you ever take home doggie bags? Why or why not?

2 Listening

The Slow Food movement

A What do members of the Slow Food movement believe? Listen and check (✓) your answer. (CD 1, Track 14)

☐ We should support and celebrate local food traditions.

☐ We should cook and serve food slowly.

☐ We should grow food slowly and carefully.

 World Link

The average French person eats 500 snails a year. Now that's an example of really "slow food"!

B Listen again. Complete the sentences with words from the box. (You will not use all the words.) (CD 1, Track 15)

| dinner | farmers | life | spicy | Europe | fast | members | the U.S. |

1. People in the Slow Food movement don't like _____ food.
2. They think we should slow down and enjoy _____.
3. They also believe in supporting local _____ and their products.
4. The Slow Food movement started in _____.
5. It has more than 65,000 _____.

ask & ANSWER

What are some advantanges of the Slow Food movement?
Can you think of any disadvantages?
Would you join the movement? Why or why not?

3 Reading

The healthiest people in the world

What is your idea of a healthy diet? What should people do to keep healthy?

A Read the article about the lifestyle of Okinawans on page 19. Then complete the chart below.

Okinawan Centenarians

What they eat	What they drink	How they exercise	How they relax
fresh fruits	_____	_____	_____
_____			

The Healthiest Lifestyle in the World?

In many countries around the world, people are living
5 longer than before. People have healthier lifestyles, and healthcare is
10 better, too.

Okinawa is an island off the coast of Japan. The people on Okinawa, the Okinawans, may have the longest lives and healthiest lifestyles in the world.

15 Researchers did a study. They started their study by looking at city and town birth records from 1879. They didn't expect to find many centenarians in the records. They were very surprised to find so many old and healthy people living in
20 Okinawa. The United States, for example, has 10 centenarians per 100,000 people. In Okinawa there are 34 centenarians per 100,000 people!

What is the Okinawans' secret?
25 First, they eat a healthy diet. They eat many fresh fruits and vegetables. They also eat fish often and drink a lot of water and green tea. But researchers think that the Okinawans have other healthy habits as
30 well. They don't do hard exercise such as weight lifting or jogging—instead, they prefer relaxing activities like gardening and walking. Researchers say that older Okinawans also have a good attitude about
35 aging. They sit quietly and relax their minds with deep breathing exercises. They also enjoy massage.

■ ■ ■ ■ ■ ■ ■ ■ ■ ■ ■ ■ ■ ■ ■

 B **Find these words in the reading.**

1. Find a word in line 8 that means *ways of living:* <u>lifestyles</u>
2. Find a word in line 15 that means *people who study something:* _____
3. *Century* means *100 years.* Find a word in line 18 that means *people who have lived 100 years or more:* _____
4. Find a word in line 30 that means *things that you do often:* _____
5. Find a word in line 35 that means *the way you feel about something:* _____

 ask**&** ANSWER

Why do Okinawans live so long? Give some reasons.
What other people in the world have healthy lifestyles? Why do you think so?
Do people in your country have healthy lifestyles? Give examples.

The superlative form of adjectives

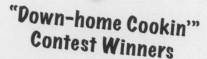

**"Down-home Cookin'"
Contest Winners**

The award for **the most unusual** dish went to Abel Cook of San Antonio, Texas. Anita Salt won for **the tastiest meal** on a budget. The grand prize went to Alfredo Fettucini for **the most delicious** meal of all.

Congratulations to all the winners!

A Read the announcement. Notice the form of the adjectives in blue. Then answer the questions.

1. What's the name of the contest?
2. What do you think the name means?
3. What kinds of foods do you think might be entered in this contest?

B Look at the chart and fill in the missing words. Then check your answers with a partner.

The superlative form of adjectives					
One syllable		**Two syllables**		**Three or more syllables**	
_____	the sweetest	simple	_____	relaxing	the most relaxing
large	_____	spicy	_____	delicious	_____
big	the biggest	crowded	the most crowded	interesting	_____

C Read about these eating places. Fill in the superlative form of the adjectives in parentheses.

Everyone is rushing to Lulu's! *City Dining* magazine says it is ___the trendiest___ (trendy) and _____ (romantic) new dinner spot. Call early—it's also _____ (difficult) place to get a reservation, because it's _____ (popular) place around!

JJ's Jazz Joint is _____ (noisy) and _____ (exciting) place to visit on a Friday night. It has _____ (good) entertainment. JJ's has _____ (large) jazz band in the city and _____ (cheap) food and drinks.

D Pair work. Work with a partner. Use these adjectives to talk about restaurants you know.

noisy	trendy	cheap
boring	romantic	bad

Bob's Bistro is the noisiest restaurant I know.

5 Writing

Restaurant review

 A You are a restaurant reviewer for a popular website.
Choose a restaurant and make some notes. Then write a review.

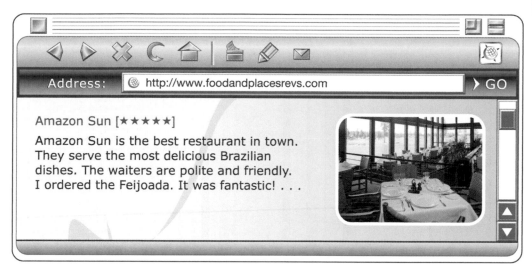

Address: http://www.foodandplacesrevs.com ➤ GO

Amazon Sun [★★★★★]

Amazon Sun is the best restaurant in town.
They serve the most delicious Brazilian
dishes. The waiters are polite and friendly.
I ordered the Feijoada. It was fantastic! . . .

Restaurant: Amazon Sun

Food: Brazilian

Price: Moderate

Location: Downtown

Service: Polite and friendly

 B Pair work. Read your partner's review. Decide if you want to try the restaurant.

6 Communication

Comparing foods

A Complete this chart with foods you know.

Spicy foods	Sweet foods	Expensive foods	Traditional foods

B Pair work. Compare your list with a partner's.
Tell your partner which food you think is . . .

I think tiramisu is the most delicious food on the list.

the most delicious   the most exotic   the hardest to prepare at home

the cheapest to buy   the healthiest   the worst for you

C Group work. Work in small groups. Create a menu for a new restaurant using many of the foods your group's members have written. Divide the menu into sections (appetizers, entrees, drinks, desserts). Include prices.

D Post your menus for the class to see.

 Check out the World Link video.   **Practice your English online at worldlink.heinle.com.**

Unsolved Mysteries

Lesson A | A detective is on the case.

1 Vocabulary Link

Cops and robbers

 A Group work. Use each verb with a noun to make eight expressions. Write the expressions on the lines below. Some of the nouns will be used more than once.

Verbs			Nouns		
~~arrest~~	catch	question	an alibi	a law	a crime
break	have	solve	a confession	a criminal	
commit	make				

arrest a criminal   D

_____ __ _____ __ _____ __

_____ __ _____ __

B Look at the expressions in A. Which actions does a police detective do? Which ones does a criminal do? Label the actions *D* (detective) or *C* (criminal).

C Look at the pictures. What is happening? Make at least two sentences about each picture. Use expressions from A.

A Look at the photo. Who is this famous detective? Where is he from? Why is he famous?

B Listen and check (✓) the box of each correct answer. (CD 1, Track 16)

1. What was Sir Arthur Conan Doyle's first job?

   ☐ actor ☐ writer ☐ doctor

2. When was the first Sherlock Holmes story published?

   ☐ 1877 ☐ 1878 ☐ 1887

3. Holmes was very _____.

   ☐ intelligent ☐ strong ☐ quick

4. Who did Holmes work with?

   ☐ Dr. Samson ☐ Dr. Watson ☐ Dr. Smith

5. Where is the Sherlock Holmes Museum?

   ☐ Scotland ☐ England ☐ the United States

ask&
ANSWER

Talk about a famous detective you know from TV, movies, or books. Why is the detective special? How does he or she solve crimes?

3 Pronunciation

Third person singular in the present tense

A Does the verb in each sentence end in the sound /s/, the sound /z/, or the sound /ɪz/? Check (✓) the box you think is correct.

	the sound /s/	the sound /z/	the sound /ɪz/
1. That man seems angry.	☐	☐	☐
2. She speaks French.	☐	☐	☐
3. Your sister looks tired.	☐	☐	☐
4. He practices the piano every day.	☐	☐	☐
5. My aunt always watches the news.	☐	☐	☐
6. My friend knows the answer.	☐	☐	☐

B Listen and check your answers. Then practice saying the sentences. (CD 1, Track 17)

4 Speaking

The Dodd Diamond

 A Listen to the conversation between Detectives Stye and Frye.
Then practice the conversation with a partner. (CD 1, Track 18)

Stye: Do you know the Dodd Diamond?

Frye: Of course! The museum owns it.

Stye: Not anymore! Someone stole it last night!

Frye: Really? How did it happen?

Stye: Well, it's unlikely the criminal walked into the room.
There's an alarm on the floor.

Frye: But there's no alarm for the skylight.

Stye: You're right! I bet the criminal climbed down a rope.
Then he took the diamond without touching the floor!

B How did the criminal steal the diamond? Number the
steps from 1 to 4.

☐ He climbed down the rope.　　☐ He threw down a rope.

☐ He opened the skylight.　　☐ He stole the diamond.

5 Speaking Strategy

Talking about possibility

A Write + beside the expressions that describe something more than 50 percent possible. Write — beside
the ones that describe something less than 50 percent possible. Check your answers with a partner.

1. __+__ It's likely (that) . . .　　　4. _____ It doesn't seem possible (that) . . .

2. _____ I doubt (that) . . .　　　5. _____ It's unlikely (that) . . .

3. _____ I bet (that) . . .　　　6. _____ There's a good chance (that) . . .

B On a piece of paper, write six statements about yourself.
Some of the statements should be true and some should be
false. Mix up your statements.

C Pair work. Take turns reading the statements to your partner.
Your partner should say whether each statement seems
possible or not. Give reasons for your answers.

I love chocolate.

*There's a good chance that's true.
I know you like sweets. You probably
like chocolate, too.*

1. I love chocolate.

2. My family moved three times.

3. I own 300 CDs.

4. I . . .

6 Language Link

Stative verbs

A Look at the chart of stative verbs below. Then add verbs in the box to the chart.

> hate   hear   like   own   smell   understand

Stative Verbs

Thinking verbs	Having verbs	Feeling verbs	Sensing verbs	Other verbs
believe	belong	appreciate	_____	seem
know	have	_____	see	look
think	_____	_____	_____	mean
_____		love	taste	cost
				need

B These sentences use stative verbs. The sentences in Column A are correct. The ones in Column B are incorrect. What can you say about stative verbs?

Column A (correct)	Column B (incorrect)
I own more than 100 CDs.	~~I am owning more than 100 CDs.~~
We know many words in English.	~~We are knowing many words in English.~~
This book belongs on the shelf.	~~This book is belonging on the shelf.~~

C A detective (D) is reporting back to police headquarters (HQ). Write each verb in the simple present or present continuous. Check your answers with a partner.

HQ: What do you see?

D: Right now, I <u>'m looking</u> (look) down an alley. Everything _____ (seem) quiet. Wait a minute! I _____ (see) a tall man. He _____ (eat) something. It _____ (look) like a candy bar.

HQ: What's he doing now?

D: OK, now he _____ (read) a piece of paper. He _____ (talk) to himself. He _____ (seem) confused.

HQ: Do you see anything now?

D: I _____ (see) another man. He's short. He _____ (have) an object in his hand. Oh, no! It's a gun! I _____ (need) some help!

World Link

Valued at U.S. $100 million, the *Mona Lisa* may be the most expensive item ever stolen. It was taken from the Louvre museum in 1911 and recovered in Italy in 1913.

7 Communication

The Lindbergh kidnapping

 Pair work. Read this true story. With a partner, brainstorm any questions that come to mind.

Charles Lindbergh was a famous pilot. He was the first man to fly solo across the Atlantic Ocean. Anne Lindbergh was his wife. They were very rich. On the cold night of March 1, 1932, someone kidnapped their baby from their home. The kidnapper used a ladder. The person wrote a note and asked for $50,000.

What time did the crime happen?

 There were many people involved in the Lindbergh case. Read each profile. Which people seem suspicious to you?

Charles and Anne Lindbergh
Someone kidnapped their baby. Charles was a reserved man. Anne was shy and quiet.

Violet Sharpe
She was one of the Lindbergh's maids. She was not in the house on March 1. She was sad and unhealthy. She drank poison and died.

Ernie Brinkert
He was Violet's boyfriend. He knew about the Lindberghs. His handwriting didn't match the kidnapper's note.

Bruno Hauptmann
He was a carpenter. Detectives found money in his house. He had a ladder.

Betty Gow
She was one of the Lindbergh's maids. She was the last person to see the baby. She loved the baby. She fainted at the trial.

Amandus Hochmuth
He was 87 years old. He was the Lindbergh's neighbor. He saw Bruno in a car near the Lindbergh mansion.

 Pair work. Which person possibly committed the crime? Who definitely didn't do it? Work with a partner. On a sheet of paper, write down your ideas about each person and your reasons.

Group work. Join another pair and tell them your ideas. Try to convince them you are right.

It's unlikely that Betty Gow did it. She loved the baby.

Unsolved Mysteries

Lesson B | Mysteries of the world

1 Vocabulary Link

It's puzzling!

A Look at the computer game. Then read the back cover of the package. Can you guess the meaning of the words in red?

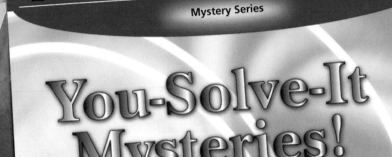

X Station by TECPal

Mystery Series

You-Solve-It Mysteries!

This new computer game is truly interactive. You can solve over 10 **puzzling** mysteries yourself or with friends! Here are some examples:

- On January 1, 2000, Missy Smith left her home and never returned—she simply **vanished**. Hear the **testimony** of her friends and family. What do you think happened?
- Three scary **legends** about ghosts—do you think the stories are true?
- Do you believe in UFOs or are they one big **hoax**? What **proof** or **evidence** do we have?

People have many **weird** experiences in their lives. "You-Solve-It Mysteries!" tells us all about them.

 You can find the answers to these mystifying stories!

B Match the underlined words in A with the words with a similar meaning below. Use each word only once.

1. confusing _____ mystifying, puzzling _____
2. true statement _____
3. clue _____
4. disappeared _____
5. strange _____
6. old stories _____
7. trick _____

ask **&** ANSWER

Would you buy the computer game in A? Why or why not?

2 Listening

Strange lights

> Imagine that you see some strange lights in the sky.
> What would you do? How would you feel?

A Listen to this news report. What did Nick Brown do? Number the steps 1 to 5. (CD 1, Track 19)

_____ tried to take pictures

__1__ drove down the highway

_____ told a police officer

_____ called his wife

_____ saw the lights

B Listen again. Who saw the lights? Check (✓) the boxes. (CD 1, Track 20)

☐ Nick Brown ☐ police officer ☐ Mike ☐ local people ☐ Alexa

3 Reading

The Marfa mystery lights

> What do you think causes mysterious lights in the sky?
> ☐ lightning ☐ UFOs ☐ stars ☐ car headlights ☐ other: _____

A Read the interview with Dr. Raj, an expert on the Marfa mystery lights, on page 29.
Then write the questions below in the correct boxes in the reading.

a. ~~What are the mystery lights exactly?~~

b. What do the experts say?

c. Are the local people scared?

d. Some people say they are car headlights. Do you think so?

e. What are some of the weirdest ideas about the lights?

f. Where is Marfa and what exactly is it famous for?

B The statements below are incorrect. Find a sentence from the reading
to show why each statement is incorrect and write it on the line.

1. "The Marfa mystery lights look the same to everyone."
   Different people see different lights.

2. "Robert Ellison saw the lights ninety years ago."
   _____

3. "The native Americans thought that ball lightning caused the lights."
   _____

4. "A team from Japan solved the mystery."
   _____

DOCTOR RAJ DISCUSSES "MYSTERY LIGHTS"

Q: 1.

A: Marfa is a small town in west Texas in the United States. It's famous for the "Marfa mystery lights."

Q: 2. What are the mystery lights exactly?

A: No one knows for sure. There are many different ideas about that.

Q: Can you describe them?

A: That's a difficult question. Different people see different lights. They are not always the same. I can say that they appear after sunset in the sky. They dance mysteriously in the air and vanish. Then they suddenly reappear.

Q: 3.

A: No, I don't. A man first saw the mystery lights over 100 years ago. The man was Robert Ellison and the year was 1883. Of course we didn't have cars in 1883!

Q: What do you think causes the lights?

A: There are many theories. The Native Americans thought the lights were stars falling to Earth. Some people think uranium gas causes the lights. Other people suggest that ball lightning does it. Ball lightning is lightning in the shape of a circle. It often appears just after a rainstorm.

Q: 4.

A: Well, some people call them the "ghost lights." They think ghosts do it. That's the strangest idea. Some say they are UFOs. I don't think so.

Q: 5.

A: They can't figure it out. Some engineers even came from Japan one time. They studied the lights, but couldn't solve the mystery.

Q: 6.

A: No, actually, they aren't. They like the lights. And every year in early September there's a big town festival to celebrate the mystery lights.

World Link

The world's only UFO landing pad was built in 1967 in Alberta, Canada. It's never been used—so far . . .

ask & ANSWER

What do you think causes the "Marfa mystery lights"?
Do you know any other stories about strange lights in the sky?

4

Language Link

Adverbs of manner

A Use the adverbs of manner to complete the story.
Use each adverb only once.

calmly	neatly	slowly
clearly	nervously	strangely
happily	quickly	
~~heavily~~	quietly	

It was raining h**eavily**____. I couldn't see c_____. I drove s_____. Suddenly, I saw a young girl. She was dressed n_____ and standing in the middle of the road. I was surprised! Somehow, I stopped the car q_____.

"What are you doing?" I asked. She looked at me s_____ but didn't answer. "Are you OK?" I asked. "I'm fine," she answered. Then she smiled h_____ and walked away q_____.

N_____, I drove to my hotel and checked in. I told the clerk about the little girl. "Do you know her?" I asked. "Oh yes," he said c_____. "That's Mary Anne. She died five years ago on that road. It was a car accident during a rainstorm."

B Look at the story in A again.
Then circle the words to complete the sentences.

1. Adverbs of manner tell you how / why something is done.
2. Adverbs of manner usually come before / after the verb.
3. Adverbs of manner often end in -ed / -ly.

> Remember! Stative verbs (be, look, hear, etc.) are followed by an adjective.

C Circle the adjective or the adverb to complete the sentences.

1. Look careful / (carefully) at the evidence.
2. That's a strange / strangely clue.
3. The figure disappeared quick / quickly.
4. Something smells strange / strangely in here.
5. You seem quiet / quietly today. Are you OK?
6. She speaks French fluent / fluently.
7. He's 90, but he still hears good / well.
8. Drive slow / slowly and be careful / carefully.

D Pair work. Retell the story of Mary Anne in your own words to a partner. Don't look at the story.

Writing

A strange event

A Write a story for your local newspaper about an unsolved mystery or strange event. Use adverbs of manner.

B Pair work. Exchange papers with a partner. Add one or two adverbs of manner to your partner's story.

Mr. Hobbs was a farmer. One night there was a loud noise. It was 2 a.m. and Mr. Hobbs woke up. It was dark and he couldn't see clearly. He turned on a light. He could see his fields. They were cut strangely. They all looked like circles! The next day Mr. Hobbs calmly told the police his story. The police . . .

6 Communication

It's a big hoax.

A Look at these unsolved mysteries. Check (✓) if you think it is real, a hoax, or you are not sure. Write your reasons.

the Marfa mystery lights

1. ☐ real ✓ hoax ☐ not sure
   Maybe they're caused by ball
   lightning or uranium gas.

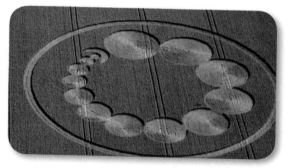

crop circles

2. ☐ real ☐ hoax ☐ not sure
   _____
   _____

the Loch Ness monster

3. ☐ real ☐ hoax ☐ not sure
   _____
   _____

scary ghosts

4. ☐ real ☐ hoax ☐ not sure
   _____
   _____

B Pair work. Compare your answers with a partner. Then together choose one of the mysteries that you both think is a hoax. Describe how you think the hoax was done. Use adverbs of manner in your description.

C Group work. Present your ideas to another pair.

ask&
ANSWER
Many mysteries are proven to be hoaxes. Why do you think people still like to believe in them? Can you think of an example?

 Check out the World Link video.   **Practice your English online at** worldlink.heinle.com.

1 Storyboard

A Susan, Maya, and Bruno work for an international trading company. Look at the pictures and complete the conversations. For some blanks, more than one answer is possible.

_____? I don't know him.

That's Bruno Cardoso. He's from the Rio de Janeiro office.

① Rio? That's interesting.

Hi, Bruno. _____.

② It's good to see you again, too, Maya.

Bruno, _____ Susan Park.

Later that day . . .

③ _____, Susan. I'm Bruno Cardoso.

_____, Bruno.

④ Well, I'm almost finished for the day.

Great! _____ dinner?

I'm sorry. _____ seafood.

⑤ Seafood

_____ that new seafood place?

OK, then _____ a French restaurant?

⑥ _____. I love French food.

Me too! Let's leave the office at 6:15.

B Group work. Practice the conversations. Then change roles and practice again.

C Group work. Introduce a friend to another friend. Invite both friends out to dinner.

2 See it and say it

 A Look at the 1994 yearbook photos for these students.

1. In 1994, what year were they in school:
   senior, junior, sophomore, or freshman?
2. What activities did each student participate in?

Rachel,
Thanks for being
my friend. See
you next year.
Levan

Anna Lopez
Class of 1994
Yearbook Club

Rachel Williams
Class of 1996
Cheerleader

Levan Brown
Class of 1995
Spanish Club

Matt Chester
Class of 1997
Soccer Team

Hamilton High School Yearbook 1994

B Look at the people in A as they are today.

1. What are their relationships today?
2. What are they doing in each picture?
3. What else can we say about them? Make up a story for one of the pictures.

Matt and Anna

Rachel and Levan

3 Listening: Who ate the cake?

 A Listen to the people talk about different foods. What kind of foods does each person like? Write the answers under the pictures. (CD 1, Track 21)

 Adam

 Janet

 Abby

 Minh

1. _____ foods   2. _____ foods   3. _____ foods   4. _____ foods

 B Pair work. Which person in A has eaten each of the foods below? Talk about the possibilities.

> I doubt that Minh ate the chocolate cake. He only eats healthy foods.

C Pair work. What kinds of foods do you like? Which person are you most like? Tell your partner.

4 I'm reading an interesting book.

 A Choose three words from the box. Write three sentences about yourself in your notebook. Use the simple present or the present continuous.

> eat   know   like   study
> read   own   work

B Group work. Take turns. Read one of your sentences. Each person in the group asks a question about your sentence.

A: I always eat cereal for breakfast.
B: What kind of cereal do you eat?
A: Wheat flakes.
C: Why do you always eat cereal?
A: I don't have time in the morning. It's quick and easy.

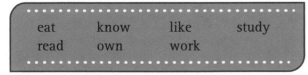

5 Man-made wonders of the world

Use the adjectives in the box to ask and answer questions about these monuments.

beautiful	interesting	popular	strange
impressive	old	remote	tall

The Great Wall of China

The statues on Easter Island

The Eiffel Tower

The Roman Colosseum

Which monument is the oldest?

Well, the statues on Easter Island look old, but I think the Roman Colosseum is older.

6 Act it out.

A Group work. With your group, add two more verbs and adverbs to the chart.

Verbs		Adverbs	
climb	sing	calmly	nervously
dance	_____	carefully	quickly
laugh	_____	gracefully	quietly
run		happily	_____
		terribly	_____

You're singing terribly.

B Group work. Choose an action verb from the left and an adverb from the right. Then act out the verb/adverb combination. Can your group guess the answer?

4 Today's Trends

Lesson A | Modern family trends

1 Vocabulary Link

Family statistics

A Use the expressions to complete the statistics about American families.

1. a majority of
2. 15 percent
3. quadrupled
4. four times
5. two thirds

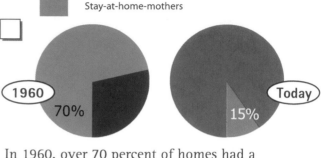

Stay-at-home-mothers

1960 — 70%

Today — 15%

a. In 1960, over 70 percent of homes had a working father and a stay-at-home mother. Today, this is true for only **15 percent** of homes.

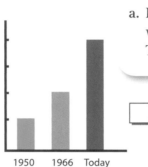

1950 1966 Today

b. The number of divorces today is twice as high as in 1966 and _____ as high as in 1950.

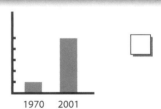

1970 2001

c. The number of unmarried couples living together _____ from 1970 to 2001.

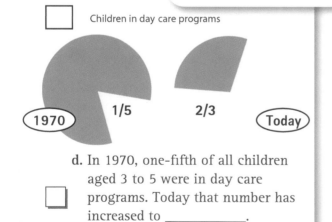

Children in day care programs

1970   1/5   2/3   Today

d. In 1970, one-fifth of all children aged 3 to 5 were in day care programs. Today that number has increased to _____.

Believe

Do not believe

e. _____ women believe both men and women should work outside the home, and that both should help with the children.

B Pair work. What do you think of the statistics in A? Write + (positive trend) or − (negative trend) in the boxes. Discuss your answers with a partner.

I think that the first statistic is a positive trend for women.

ask**&**
ANSWER

Which statistics surprise you? Why?
How are American families similar to families in your country? How are they different?

2 Listening

Non-traditional families

 A Listen to interviews with two families and check (✓) the appropriate box or boxes. (CD 1, Track 22)

Interview 1

	takes care of the baby	goes to work every day
Dan	☐	☐
Courtney	☐	☐

Interview 2

	takes care of the girls	works at home
Jamal	☐	☐
Tia	☐	☐

 B Listen again. Check (✓) *True* or *False*. (CD 1, Track 23)

	True	False			True	False
1. Courtney is a manager.	☐	☐	3. Jamal and Tia are writers.		☐	☐
2. Dan is a house husband.	☐	☐	4. They have a baby.		☐	☐

ask&
ANSWER

What do you think about being a house husband?
Do you know any non-traditional families?

3 Pronunciation

Unstressed *of* in rapid speech

 A Listen. Notice the pronunciation of the word *of*. (CD 1, Track 24)

1. All of the families live in big cities.
2. None of the students study German.
3. Some of the people don't agree with me.

Note: In rapid speech, the final *f* sound in *of* is usually dropped before a consonant sound.

 B Listen and complete the sentences. Then practice saying them aloud. (CD 1, Track 25)

1. _____ the young children are in day care.
2. _____ their parents work two or three jobs.
3. _____ my friends grew up in the same town.
4. _____ my classmates like to study.

4 Speaking

I don't agree!

 A **Read the statistic below. What do you think of this trend?**

A day care center is a place where children are cared for while their parents are at work. Today in the United States, over two-thirds of children aged 3 to 5 are in a day care center or preschool program.

 B **Listen to two politicians discussing the statistic above. Do they agree or disagree about the issue?** (CD 1, Track 26)

Moderator:	Good evening, ladies and gentlemen. Welcome to our debate. Mr. Taylor, please begin.
Mr. Taylor:	We have a big problem. Too many children are in day care centers. This is not good.
Moderator:	Ms. Marin, what do you think?
Ms. Marin:	I'm a mother and I work. In today's society, most mothers and fathers are busy with work.
Moderator:	So they don't have a choice? They need day care?
Ms. Marin:	Exactly. And it's very expensive.
Moderator:	What can we do about this situation?
Mr. Taylor:	We can encourage mothers and fathers to stay at home with their children.
Ms. Marin:	I don't agree. I think we should try to offer cheaper day care.

 C **Group work. Practice the conversation in groups of three.**

> **Useful Expressions:**
> **Disagreeing**
>
> I don't agree.
> I don't think so.
> I disagree.
> I don't think that's true.
> Not necessarily.

5 Speaking Strategy 🛠

Expressing disagreement

 A **Read the statements. Check (✓) Agree or Disagree and write a reason.**

1. It's wonderful that working parents can put their children in day care.
   [✓] Agree [ ] Disagree   Reason: <u>Both the husband and wife can work and make more money.</u>

2. Especially in a family with young children, only one parent should work.
   [ ] Agree [ ] Disagree   Reason: _____

3. A father can never match a mother in taking care of children and the home.
   [ ] Agree [ ] Disagree   Reason: _____

4. Couples are getting married too late these days.
   [ ] Agree [ ] Disagree   Reason: _____

 B **Pair work. Take turns reading the statements in A. Your partner agrees or disagrees with the statement, then says the reason.**

> *It's wonderful that working parents can put their children in day care.*

> *I don't think so. Young children need their parents.*

6 Language Link

Quantity expressions

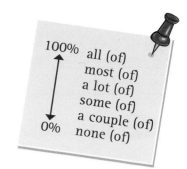

100% all (of)
most (of)
a lot (of)
some (of)
a couple (of)
0% none (of)

A Read the information about six families from around the world.
Then write *all, most, a lot, some, a couple,* or *none* in the blanks below.

	the SHAW family	the IKEDA family	the OLIVEIRA family	the CHOI family	the POPOV family	the KUMAR family
hometown	Chicago	Tokyo	São Paulo	Seoul	Moscow	New Delhi
language	English	Japanese	Portuguese	Korean	Russian	English
housing	house	apartment	apartment	apartment	apartment	apartment
transportation	car	subway	bus	car	car	bus
wife works	restaurant	office	hotel	office	office	office
children	no	yes	yes	yes	yes	yes

1. _____ of the families live in big cities.
2. _____ of the families speak English.
3. _____ of them speak French.
4. _____ live in apartments.
5. _____ travel by car.
6. _____ of the families have a working wife.
7. _____ of the wives work in an office.
8. _____ of the families have children.

B Pair work. Tell your partner about the families you know using *all (of), most (of), a lot (of), some (of), a couple (of),* or *none (of).* Use the list below.

have children   have pets
have a stay-at-home wife   have a house husband

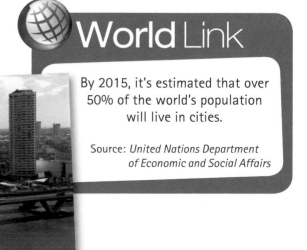

World Link

By 2015, it's estimated that over
50% of the world's population
will live in cities.

Source: *United Nations Department
of Economic and Social Affairs*

Lesson A • Modern family trends   **39**

A Read the opinions of the people below. Do you agree or disagree?
Check (✓) *Agree* or *Disagree* and write a reason for each one.

"You always have to think of yourself first."

"The secret to success is to stay with the same company throughout your career."

"Our children's lives will be better than ours in many ways."

1. ☐ Agree ☐ Disagree
Reason: _____
_____

2. ☐ Agree ☐ Disagree
Reason: _____
_____

3. ☐ Agree ☐ Disagree
Reason: _____
_____

B Group work. Get into groups of six to eight.
Discuss your answers with the members of your group.

C Group work. Survey the members of your group. Find out how many agree and how
many disagree with the modern opinions about life and work in the chart below.

Modern opinions about life and work	How many agree?	How many disagree?
1. Life is hard and there are no guarantees of success.		
2. It is better to get married later in life.		
3. The most important person to trust is yourself.		
4. It is important to have a balance between work life and home life.		
5. The future will be positive.		
6. Life for my generation will be better than it was for my parents' generation.		
7. You shouldn't change jobs more than once or twice in your lifetime.		

D Class activity. Report your results back to the class. Discuss the results as a class.

All of the people in my group think it's important to have a balance between work life and home life.

A couple of my group's members feel it's better to get married later in life.

Today's Trends

Lesson B | In style

1 Vocabulary Link

I want to be trendy!

A Marissa had a *makeover*. She got new clothes, a new hairstyle, and a great new look.
Read about the company that did it. Notice the words in red.

A New You! Inc.

We have **innovative** ideas and offer **outstanding** customer service. Our makeovers are **tailor-made** for you! Our goal: to give you an **individual** sense of style. We **follow** the latest trends, so you don't have to!

See for yourself!

Before

"I love my new look! Before I looked very old-fashioned. Now I'm so stylish!"

After

B Match the definitions in the box with the words below.

appearance	excellent	~~new and creative~~	not modern
fashionable	study; watch	personal	for a particular person

1. innovative (*adj.*) __new and creative__
2. outstanding (*adj.*) _____
3. tailor-made (*adj.*) _____
4. individual (*adj.*) _____

5. follow (*v.*) _____
6. look (*n.*) _____
7. old-fashioned (*adj.*) _____
8. stylish (*adj.*) _____

ask **&**
ANSWER

What kinds of things are old-fashioned?
What is innovative or stylish?
Would you like to have a makeover?
Why or why not?

World Link

Brazilians are the world's most enthusiastic shoppers. In one survey, more than 80% said they love or like shopping for clothes.

Source: *Cotton Incorporated's Lifestyle Monitor™*

2 Listening

What's your personal style?

 A Listen to these interviews on the street in New York.
Where are these people from? Write down their hometowns. (CD 1, Track 27)

Gio

Elena

Vicki

	Gio	Elena	Vicki
Hometown?	Milan		
Clothes from?			
Personal style?		retro	

  B Listen again. Complete the rest of the chart. (CD 1, Track 28)

ask**&**
ANSWER

How would you describe your individual sense of style?
Are you interested in trends in music or fashion? Why or why not?

3 Reading

Trendspotting

A Read the advertisement.
What do you think a
trendspotter does?
Who would hire
a trendspotter?

Are you between the ages of 15 and 22? Do you
like fashion and music? Do you know what's hot?
You could be a trendspotter! We are looking
for young people who have opinions about
trends and who like to have fun!

- Try new products!

- Participate in surveys!

- Receive free samples!

We want to hear your opinions!

Call now: 555-2200.

B Brooke is 18 years old. She works as a trendspotter.
What does she do? Read her diary entry.

March 17
Today I started my new part-time job as a trendspotter. I was nervous and didn't know what to expect. Well, guess what? It was a lot of fun! I'm telling all my friends, "You should think about becoming a trendspotter, too!"

On Saturday morning, we had to report to a recording studio by 10 a.m. The "Trends Coordinator," Mandy, explained the schedule. Then she gave us a tour. That was really cool!

Next we sat around a big table in a room. They gave each person three cards. One card said "Yes—All the way!" Another said, "It's OK." The third one said, "No way!" We listened to about 10 different songs. After each song we had to hold up a card. They played some hip hop, rock, heavy metal, and dance music. The heavy metal was "No way" for me!

Do you know the rock group called "Gifted"? They're really popular right now. Well, they have a new CD coming out. We saw six different CD covers. (I guess they are trying to choose one.) This time, we didn't have any cards. Instead, we just talked about the covers we liked. Mandy asked us questions: "Which ones do you like?" "Why do you like them?" "Would you buy a CD with this cover?"

We finished at 12:30. We meet again next week at a boutique downtown. We will look at some new fashions. Each week we go to a different location. Oh yes, we also received a free CD for our work. This "job" doesn't pay, but we get free stuff!

That's all for now!

C Make the sentences true.

1. Brooke started her job in ~~January~~. March

2. The job has a good salary.

3. Brooke works once a month as a trendspotter.

4. Brooke saw only one CD cover for "Gifted."

5. Brooke held up an "It's OK" card for the heavy metal music.

ask**&**
ANSWER
Why do you think companies use trendspotters? Do you think it's a good idea?
Would you like to be a trendspotter? Why or why not?

Giving advice with *could, should, ought to,* and *had better*

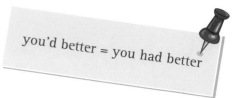
you'd better = you had better

A Read the question about cell phones and the four different answers.
Then complete the sentences with the modal verbs in blue.

Q: *I want to buy a new cell phone. What should I do?*

A1: You need some help. You **could** ask your friends or a salesperson for help.

A2: You **should** read *Consumer Advice* magazine. They rate all the different cell phone companies.

A3: You **had better** be careful. Some cell phone plans are very expensive.

A4: You**'d better not** buy a cell phone right now. The prices are too high during the holidays.

In A1, _____ is used to give a suggestion (between choices).

In A2, _____ is used to give advice. *Ought to* can also be used to give advice.

In A3, _____ is used to give stronger advice. It suggests that there may be some bad results.

In A4, the negative form of _____ sounds like a warning.

B Complete the conversations with the expressions in the boxes.
Use each expression only once.

> shouldn't   could   ought to

Betsy: I don't know what to wear to the party tonight.

Carla: You **(1)** _____ wear your new jeans or your black pants.

Betsy: It's a formal dress party.

Carla: Oh, then you **(2)** _____ wear pants after all.
You definitely **(3)** _____ wear a dress.

> had better   could   had better not

Fred: I still don't understand this grammar.

Doug: You **(4)** _____ get some help or you will fail the test. It's on Thursday.

Fred: Maybe I **(5)** _____ take the test on Friday. That would give me extra time.

Doug: Well, you **(6)** _____ delay. There's not much time!

C You are going to an informal party. Your partner is going to a formal party.
Look at the list and give advice to each other.

> arrive a little late   wear casual clothes   bring a friend who wasn't invited
> bring food for the party   wear a suit or a nice dress   bring flowers or champagne to the host

You could arrive a little late...

You shouldn't wear casual clothes...

5 Writing

You should get a makeover.

 A Read the letter from a newspaper advice column. What advice would you give Sam?

 B Now write a letter to Sad Sam. Give him advice using *should* and *shouldn't*. Share it with a partner.

Ask Susie Style

Dear Susie Style,

I need your help! I can't get a job. Everywhere I go, I get the same answer: "No!" My friend says that my appearance is the problem. Here is a picture of me. What do you think? What should I do?

Sad Sam in Seattle

6 Communication

Do you need a makeover?

 A Ask your partner the questions. Check (✓) your partner's answers.

How often do you . . .	often	sometimes	never
1. wear "the same old thing"?	☐	☐	☐
2. buy something because it's cheap?	☐	☐	☐
3. wear something comfortable but mismatched?	☐	☐	☐
4. wear something until it's completely worn out?	☐	☐	☐
5. leave the house without looking in the mirror?	☐	☐	☐
6. read fashion magazines about new trends?	☐	☐	☐
7. change your hairstyle?	☐	☐	☐
8. go to concerts and listen to new music?	☐	☐	☐

 B Calculate your partner's score. Use the table.

	for questions 1–5	for questions 6–8
often	score 2 points	score 0 points
sometimes	score 1 point	score 1 point
never	score 0 points	score 2 points

 C Read the appropriate advice to your partner. What do you think of the advice?

1–3 points: You don't need any advice. You're trendy already!	**4–7 points:** You have a good sense of style. You could change a few things or just try to do something new every week.	**8–12 points:** You could change something about your clothing or your hairstyle. You should go out more and see what's happening.	**13–16 points:** You scored a lot of points. You'd better think about getting a complete makeover!

 Check out the World Link video. **Practice your English online at** worldlink.heinle.com.

In the Neighborhood

Lesson A | Running errands

1 Vocabulary Link

A busy day

A Pair work. Work with a partner. Match the verbs with the nouns and phrases, and write the expressions in the picture. Sometimes more than one combination is possible.

Verbs		Nouns and phrases	
cut out	make	grocery shopping	a grocery list
get	pick up	the bus home	a haircut
go	take	the car at the garage	the kids from school
leave	unload	coupons	to a dentist appointment
		the dry cleaning	the groceries

Ann's errands

① cut out coupons

② _____

③ _____

④ _____

⑤ _____

⑥ _____

⑦ _____

⑧ _____

⑨ _____

⑩ _____

B Discuss these questions.

1. What errands do you do often?   2. What are some errands that are not pictured above?

2 Listening

Too much to do

How often do you listen to the radio? What kinds of programs do you listen to?

A Listen to this radio call-in show.
Write *T* (True) or *F* (False) for each statement. (CD 1, Track 29)

1. _____ The caller has enough time for his errands.

2. _____ Donna suggests an errand service.

3. _____ The caller doesn't like the suggestion.

World Link

Have a problem? Hire a *benri-ya*. In Japan, a benri-ya will do any annoying task for you, from killing a cockroach to breaking up with your boyfriend!

B Listen again. Which errands does the caller do? According to the radio host, which errands can the service do? Check (✓) the correct column(s). (CD 1, Track 30)

	Caller	Service
1. go to a doctor's appointment	☐	☐
2. take the car to the garage	☐	☐
3. pick up a child at school	☐	☐
4. go to the bank	☐	☐
5. do the grocery shopping	☐	☐

ask& ANSWER
Do you think an errand service is a good idea? Why or why not?

3 Pronunciation

Reduced forms of *could you* and *would you*

A Listen to these sentences. Notice the reduced pronunciation of *could you* and *would you* in each sentence. (CD 1, Track 31)

1. Could you open the window?
2. Would you hold the door for me? Thanks.
3. Could you answer that telephone, please?
4. Would you help me lift this box?

B Listen to these sentences. Circle the words you hear. (CD 1, Track 32)

1. That radio is awfully loud. Could you / Would you turn it down, please?
2. I think the computer is broken. Could you / Would you please look at it?
3. Oh, they're here already. Could you / Would you get the door?
4. Let me see if he's in his office. Could you / Would you hold for a moment?

C Pair work. With a partner, practice reading the sentences in B.
Use reduced forms of *could you* and *would you*.

4 Speaking

Can I help you?

 A Jim and Frida are shopping. Listen to the conversation.
Underline the words that Frida uses to get the clerk's attention. (CD 1, Track 33)

Jim:	There's no price tag on it.
Frida:	Let's ask someone for help. Excuse me, how much is this?
Woman:	I don't know. I don't work here.
Frida:	Oh, I'm sorry!
Jim:	How about that man behind the counter? Ask him.

Frida:	Excuse me, do you work here?
Man:	Yes, I do. Can I help you?
Frida:	How much does this cost?
Man:	It's $29.99.
Frida:	Great! I'll take it. Could you wrap it for me, please?
Man:	Certainly.

 B Group work. Practice the conversation in groups of four.

5 Speaking Strategy

Getting a clerk's attention in a store

 A Match each conversation to a picture below.

1. **Man:** Excuse me. Do you work here?
   Clerk: Yes, I do. Can I help you?
   Man: Yes. Where can I find the dairy section?

2. **Woman:** Are you busy? I need some help.
   Clerk: No problem.
   Woman: How much does this cost?

3. **Man:** Sorry to bother you, but I have a question.
   Clerk: OK. Go right ahead.
   Man: Which form do I use for this package?

 B Pair work. Work with a partner. Create a short conversation to role-play based on the picture.

Woman: *Excuse me . . .*

Useful Expressions:
Getting a clerk's attention
Excuse me. Do you work here?
Sorry to bother you, but I have a question.
Are you busy? I need some help.

6 Language Link

Polite requests with modal verbs and *mind*

A Study the chart. Notice the verb forms.

Making requests			
For polite, neutral, and more casual situations, use:		For polite and very polite situations, use:	
Can you Will you Could you Would you	help me please?	Would you mind	helping me please?

B Look at the two pictures. Complete the first part of each conversation.
Use the chart above to help you.

C Read these requests. Each sentence has an error. Correct it.

1. Would you mind wait here for a moment?
2. Will you please asking for directions?
3. Can you answer please the telephone?
4. Would you minding take notes for me?

D Imagine that you are in these situations. Write a request for each situation.
Use the words in parentheses.

1. It's hot. Your classmate is sitting by the window. The window is closed. (open/window)

   _____

2. You're at the bank. You forgot your pen. Your friend has a pen. (lend/pen)

   _____

3. Your roommate is going grocery shopping. (pick up/some milk)

   _____

4. You and your friend are leaving a party. You are very tired. (drive/home)

   _____

7 Communication

An errand service

A Pair work. Work with a partner. Read the ad for an errand service and fill in the missing details.

HANDY HELPERS ERRAND SERVICE

Are you too busy to _____?
No time to _____?

We want to help you with . . .

ERRAND	PRICE
grocery shopping	$35 per hour
_____	_____
_____	_____

Hours of operation: _____

Look at what this satisfied customer said!

_____
_____
_____

B Make a list of errands that you often do. How much would you pay a service to do each errand for you?

Errand	Price	Errand	Price
_____	_____	_____	_____
_____	_____	_____	_____
_____	_____	_____	_____

C Pair work. Role play.
Imagine that you are calling an errand service. Your partner works for the errand service. Ask for help with your errands. Then switch roles.

Hello. Handy Helpers Errand Service. Can I help you?

Yes, I think so. I'm very busy. I need help with my errands.

We can help you. Which errands?

Well, I need help with my groceries. Can you go grocery shopping for me?

In the Neighborhood

Lesson B | This is my neighborhood.

1 Vocabulary Link

Describing neighborhoods

 A Look at the pictures and read the descriptions. Which neighborhood do you prefer? Why?

"My town is very **pedestrian**-friendly. There are wide sidewalks, and there's not much traffic. There's a lot of **greenery**. There are two big parks near my house. Most of the houses are new, but some of the houses are **run-down**. They are quite old and need repairs."

"I live in a nice, new **high-rise** apartment building across from the **subway** station. There's a big road in front of my building, and there is some traffic **congestion**, but in general, it's a very **convenient** neighborhood. I don't like the **litter**, though—all that trash on the street."

B Complete the questionnaire about your neighborhood. Check (✓) the appropriate circles. Then describe your neighborhood to a partner.

My neighborhood is . . .

pedestrian-friendly. ☐

near a subway station. ☐

run-down in some areas. ☐

very convenient. ☐

My neighborhood has . . .

high-rise buildings. ☐

traffic congestion. ☐

a lot of greenery. ☐

a litter problem. ☐

> *My neighborhood isn't very pedestrian-friendly. The streets are wide, and it has a lot of traffic congestion.*

2 Listening

How is the neighborhood?

A Pair work. A real estate agent is a person who rents and sells homes. What questions do you think people might ask an agent when they are buying a new home?

Is the neighborhood safe? _____

_____ _____

B Listen to the conversation. Check (✓) the things that John and Dana ask the agent about. (CD 1, Track 34)

- ☐ 1. safety
- ☐ 2. shopping
- ☐ 3. litter
- ☐ 4. schools
- ☐ 5. traffic
- ☐ 6. neighbors
- ☐ 7. public transportation
- ☐ 8. parks

C Listen again. Check (✓) the statements that are true about the neighborhood. (CD 1, Track 35)

- ☐ 1. It's noisy on Saturday nights.
- ☐ 2. The supermarket is nearby.
- ☐ 3. It's easy to cross the larger streets.
- ☐ 4. The subway station is one block away.
- ☐ 5. There are no parks nearby.

World Link

Monaco is the world's most densely populated country. There are more than 16,000 people per square kilometer. Now that's a lot of neighbors!

3 Reading

Surprising neighborhoods

A In which neighborhood would you expect to find these things? Write the things in the chart.

| eagles | an old forest | narrow streets |
| mosques | donkeys | an old farmhouse |

Inwood in New York City, USA	Fes-al-Bali in Fes, Morocco

B Kyle and Farid made web pages about their neighborhoods for a class project. Read about their neighborhoods. Were your answers in A correct? Make any necessary changes.

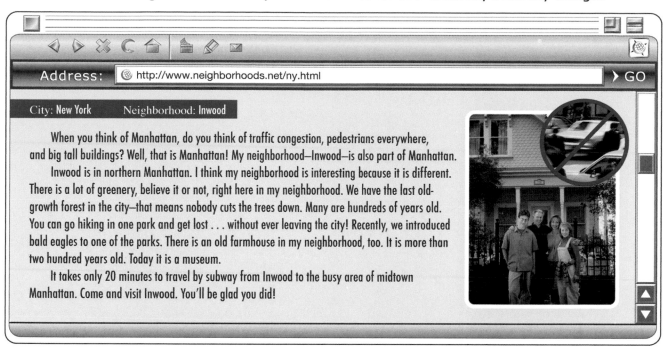

Address: http://www.neighborhoods.net/ny.html 〉GO

City: New York   Neighborhood: Inwood

When you think of Manhattan, do you think of traffic congestion, pedestrians everywhere, and big tall buildings? Well, that is Manhattan! My neighborhood—Inwood—is also part of Manhattan.

Inwood is in northern Manhattan. I think my neighborhood is interesting because it is different. There is a lot of greenery, believe it or not, right here in my neighborhood. We have the last old-growth forest in the city—that means nobody cuts the trees down. Many are hundreds of years old. You can go hiking in one park and get lost . . . without ever leaving the city! Recently, we introduced bald eagles to one of the parks. There is an old farmhouse in my neighborhood, too. It is more than two hundred years old. Today it is a museum.

It takes only 20 minutes to travel by subway from Inwood to the busy area of midtown Manhattan. Come and visit Inwood. You'll be glad you did!

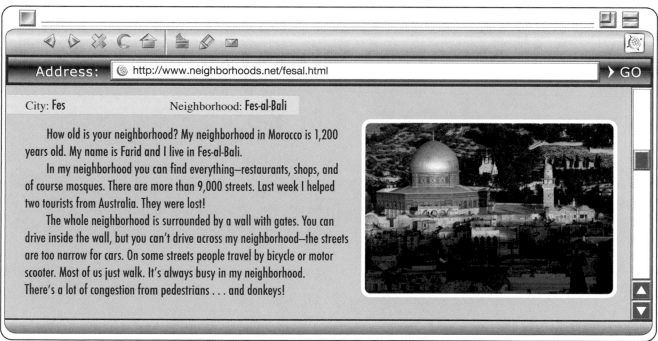

Address: http://www.neighborhoods.net/fesal.html 〉GO

City: Fes   Neighborhood: Fes-al-Bali

How old is your neighborhood? My neighborhood in Morocco is 1,200 years old. My name is Farid and I live in Fes-al-Bali.

In my neighborhood you can find everything—restaurants, shops, and of course mosques. There are more than 9,000 streets. Last week I helped two tourists from Australia. They were lost!

The whole neighborhood is surrounded by a wall with gates. You can drive inside the wall, but you can't drive across my neighborhood—the streets are too narrow for cars. On some streets people travel by bicycle or motor scooter. Most of us just walk. It's always busy in my neighborhood. There's a lot of congestion from pedestrians . . . and donkeys!

C Circle the neighborhood each sentence describes.

1. It has a farmhouse more than 200 years old.	Inwood	Fes-al-Bali
2. The neighborhood is 1,200 years old.	Inwood	Fes-al-Bali
3. It takes twenty minutes to travel to midtown.	Inwood	Fes-al-Bali
4. It has more than 9,000 streets.	Inwood	Fes-al-Bali
5. The trees are hundreds of years old.	Inwood	Fes-al-Bali

ask **&**
ANSWER

How are these neighborhoods different from yours?
Which neighborhood would you like to visit? Why?

Imperatives

A Use the verb forms below to complete the sentences.

ask	don't lose	keep	take	try
don't get lost	~~have~~	step	transfer	

1. _____Have_____ some cookies.
2. _____ your ticket on the subway. _____ it in a safe place.
3. _____ some local food. It's delicious!
4. _____ back! Here comes the train.
5. _____ the bus to City Hall. Then _____ to the subway.
6. _____ in some neighborhoods at night. _____ a police officer for help.

B Which sentence(s) in A do the following? Write the numbers of the sentences in the blanks. Some sentences may do more than one thing.

1. give advice or make suggestions _____
2. give a warning _____
3. give directions or instructions _____
4. make an offer _____

C Imagine that a visitor is coming to your neighborhood or city.
Give the visitor advice or suggestions about these topics. Use the imperative.

1. shopping: <u>Don't shop in Times Square. The stores aren't very interesting.</u>
   _____

2. transportation: _____
   _____

3. food: _____
   _____

4. local customs: _____
   _____

D Pair work. Role play. Work with a partner. One student plays the visitor and asks questions. The other answers the visitor's questions with the advice from C.

Come to my neighborhood.

A Imagine a friend is thinking of renting an apartment in your neighborhood. Write a message to him or her about the good and bad points. What makes it different or interesting?

B Pair work. Exchange messages with a partner. Decide if you'd like to live in the neighborhood.

> I live in a high-rise apartment building. It's a very noisy neighborhood. There are two big streets and a lot of traffic congestion in front of my building. There are no trees.
>
> I live there because it's convenient. The entrance to the subway station is across the street. I can get to school in less than 15 minutes by subway. A large park with lots of trees is only 20 minutes away.

Do this!

A Look at each situation. Then use one of the verbs to complete each sentence. Use the negative form for some of your answers.

| add | go | ~~keep~~ | sit |
| come | help | park | touch |

_____ the change.

_____ here.

_____ up straight.

_____ straight ahead.

Jimmy!
_____ in here!

_____ the onions.

_____ yourself.

_____ it.

B Pair work. Check your answers with a partner. Then choose one of the situations and make a short conversation about it. Be sure to use expressions from **A** in your conversation.

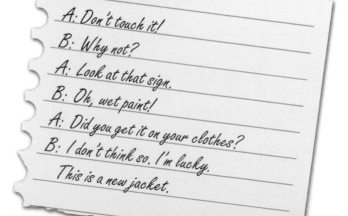
A: Don't touch it!
B: Why not?
A: Look at that sign.
B: Oh, wet paint!
A: Did you get it on your clothes?
B: I don't think so. I'm lucky. This is a new jacket.

C Perform your conversation for the class.

 Check out the World Link video. **Practice your English online at worldlink.heinle.com.**

6 Student Life

Lesson A | Starting out

1 Vocabulary Link

Applying to and starting college

 A Austin is a college student. Look at the pictures and read the sentences.

1. Austin is happy. He was **accepted** to college.

2. Austin **researched** many colleges. He decided to **apply** to four different colleges.

3. The fall **semester** is from September to December.

4. Austin **attended** college in the fall semester. He studied hard and got good **grades**.

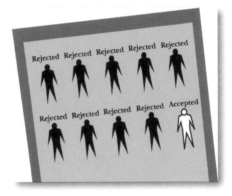

5. Austin's college is very **competitive**. Many students applied to it. Many were **rejected**.

6. His college gave him a **scholarship**. He received $5,000.

B Number the events below (1 to 6) in the order that they happened.

☐ He applied to four colleges.   ☐ He attended college in the fall semester.

☐ He got good grades.   ☐ He received a scholarship.

☐ He researched colleges.   ☐ He was accepted to college.

ask&
ANSWER

What are the names of some competitive colleges?

2 Listening

Choosing a college

 A Listen to the conversation between Kai and his high school guidance counselor. What has happened already? Check (✓) the boxes. (CD 1, Track 36)

	researched	applied to	was accepted to
California State University	☐	☐	☐
Harvard University	☐	☐	☐
City College	☐	☐	☐

 B Listen again. Match each statement to the college or university it describes. Then circle the place Kai will probably attend. (CD 1, Track 37)

1. _____ Kai visited this place before.
2. _____ It's far away.
3. _____ It's hard to get accepted there.

a. California State University
b. Harvard University
c. City College

ask**&**
ANSWER
Imagine you could study at any college or university in the world. Where would you go?

World Link

The great French painter, Paul Cézanne, applied twice for entrance to the famous Paris School of Fine Arts and was turned down both times!

3 Pronunciation

Reduced pronunciation of *going to*

 A Listen to the sentences. Notice the reduced pronunciation of *going to* in each sentence. (CD 1, Track 38)

1. I'm going to apply to three colleges.
2. He's going to clean the house next week.
3. We're going to study together for the big exam.
4. They're not going to finish in time.

 B Listen to the sentences and write the missing words you hear. (CD 1, Track 39)

1. _____ meet them before 3:00.
2. _____ take a vacation this summer.
3. _____ call us tomorrow.
4. _____ attend Harvard University.

C Tell a classmate three things you are going to do next weekend. Use the reduced pronunciation of *going to*.

What are you going to do?

I'm going to see a movie with some friends.

4 Speaking

A new high school

 A Listen to the conversation. Underline the expression Hans doesn't understand. (CD 1, Track 40)

Hans: Hi, Tom. What's new?

Tom: Well, I'm going to start at a new high school this fall.

Hans: Which one?

Tom: Essex Academy. It's a boarding school. It's a five-hour drive from my parents' house.

Hans: Does boarding school mean you live there? On campus?

Tom: Exactly.

Hans: That sounds awesome!

Tom: Yeah. I think it's going to be cool.

B Pair work. Practice the conversation with a partner.

5 Speaking Strategy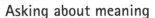

Asking about meaning

 A Pair work. Follow the instructions below.

Student A: Match the underlined words with their definitions.

> **Useful Expressions:**
> Asking about meaning
>
> Does . . . mean . . . ?
>
> What do you mean by . . . ?
>
> I don't understand.
>
> What does . . . mean?

Student A

1. ___ I study hard and get good grades. I'm usually on the <u>honor roll</u>.

2. ___ I don't live at home. I live in a <u>dormitory</u>.

3. ___ The semester ends on June 1. My <u>term paper</u> is due on May 28.

4. ___ My sister is in a <u>sorority</u> on campus. She has a lot of friends.

a. a building on campus that students live in

b. a club for female students

c. a special list for students with very good grades

d. an essay that students write at the end of a semester or term

Student B: Match the underlined words with their definitions.

Student B

1. ___ I like <u>study hall</u>. I can do my homework and prepare for exams.

2. ___ There are 300 students at my school and 25 <u>faculty</u> members.

3. ___ My <u>alma mater</u> is Oxford University. I learned a lot when I studied there.

4. ___ Jo always sleeps late and then she is <u>tardy</u> for class.

a. late (for class or an appointment)

b. all the teachers in a school, college, or university

c. a school, college, or university that you have graduated from

d. a time that is reserved for quiet study

 B Pair work. Take turns reading your sentences to your partner. Use the Useful Expressions above to ask about meaning.

I study hard and get good grades. I'm usually on the honor roll.

What does honor roll mean?

6 Language Link

Plans and decisions with *be going to* **and** *will*

A Read and practice these conversations. Then complete sentences 1 and 2 below.

Ana: I got accepted to college.
Pablo: Congratulations!
Ana: Thanks. **I'm going to attend** McGill University in the fall.

Yuri: I want to register for the grammar class.
Advisor: I'm sorry. That class is full.
Yuri: OK. **I'll register** for the writing class, then.

1. Ana uses *be going to* to express . . .

   ☐ **a.** a sudden decision.

   ☐ **b.** a decision that she made in the past.

2. Yuri uses *will ('ll)* to express . . .

   ☐ **a.** a sudden decision.

   ☐ **b.** a decision that he made in the past.

B Complete these sentences with *be going to* or *will*.

1. I got accepted to college. __I'm going to__ attend college in the fall.
2. I'm bored and don't know what to do. Wait, I know . . . I _____ read and watch TV.
3. **Waiter:** What would you like today?
   Customer: Let's see . . . I _____ have the chicken and rice, please.
4. I bought my ticket last month. I _____ visit Korea from July 1 to July 14.
5. **A:** This box is too heavy!
   B: Wait! I _____ help you.

C Read what these people are planning to do.
Make sentences using *be (not) going to*.

Eduardo

Jill

Max and Sara

☑ live at home
☐ apply for scholarships
☑ study business

☑ join a sorority
☑ do volunteer work
☐ go to a large university

☐ live in student housing
☑ study together
☑ work part-time

> *Eduardo is going to live at home.*
> *He's not going to apply for scholarships.*

 ask**&**
ANSWER
What about you? What are your future plans for school or work?

A day on campus

 A Look at the campus map. What can you do at each location?

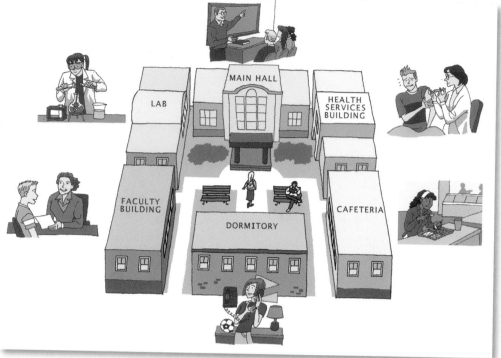

MAIN HALL

LAB

HEALTH SERVICES BUILDING

FACULTY BUILDING

DORMITORY

CAFETERIA

B Pair work. Imagine you are a student at this university. Plan a day on campus. Follow the instructions below.

Student A: Look at your schedule and fill in the remaining items from the box below.

Student B: Look at your schedule and fill in the remaining items from the box below.

Tomorrow's schedule	
10:30 a.m.	_____
12:00 p.m.	_eat lunch___
1:00 p.m.	_____
2:00 p.m.	_____
3:00 p.m.	_____
6:00 p.m.	_____
7:30 p.m.	_____

Tomorrow's schedule	
10:30 a.m.	_____
12:00 p.m.	_____
1:00 p.m.	_eat lunch___
2:00 p.m.	_____
3:00 p.m.	_____
6:00 p.m.	_____
7:30 p.m.	_____

- get a flu shot
- go to science class
- eat dinner

- study in library
- meet with English teacher
- eat dinner

C Pair work. There is a big test next week. You and your partner want to study together. Find a time tomorrow when you are both free.

> *Are you free at noon tomorrow?*

> *No, I'm not. I'm going to eat lunch with my friends then. How about 1:00?*

Student Life

Lesson B | After graduation

Definite and indefinite future time expressions

 A Look at what these students say about their graduation plans. Notice the time expressions. Which person is graduating at a definite time? Which expressions are used for indefinite time?

I'm going to graduate the day after tomorrow. I can't wait!

One of these days I'm going to graduate. Then I can go surfing every day!

 B Make a list of things you plan to do in the future. Write two things planned for a definite time and two for an indefinite time.

Definite	Indefinite
finish my homework	

C Pair work. Use the expressions below. Tell your partner about your plans.

Time Expressions	
Definite	**Indefinite**
tomorrow	one of these days
the day after tomorrow	someday
in a few days	sometime
next week	sooner or later
the week after next	in the future
next summer	
next year	

I'm going to finish my homework assignment tomorrow.

Sooner or later, I'm going to clean out my bedroom closet. It's a mess!

2 Listening

After you graduate

> What do *freshman, sophomore, junior,* and *senior* mean?
> What do you call them in your country?

A Listen to the news report. What question is the reporter, Jason Kim, asking the students? (CD 1, Track 41)

_____ after you graduate?

B Listen again. Complete the chart with information about Mizuki and Robert. (CD 1, Track 42)

	Mizuki	Robert
Major		
After graduation		

ask & ANSWER

Is it good to start a job right after you graduate? Why or why not?

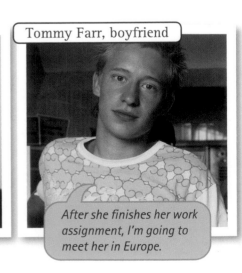

World Link

France is now the world's most popular tourist destination. However, China is expected to top the list by 2020 with a predicted 137 million visitors per year!

Source: *The UNESCO Courier*

3 Reading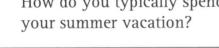

How I plan to spend my summer vacation

> How do you typically spend your summer vacation?

A The people below are talking about Stephanie. Read what they say. What do you think Stephanie is going to do this summer?

Mrs. Lee, mother

She's going to travel alone for three months. It's a great opportunity!

Mr. Lee, father

This is a perfect job for her. She loves to take photos and meet new people.

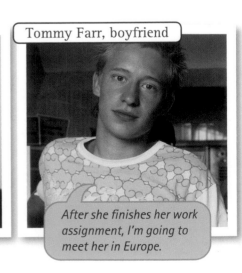

Tommy Farr, boyfriend

After she finishes her work assignment, I'm going to meet her in Europe.

B Now read the web page. Was your guess about her summer plans correct?

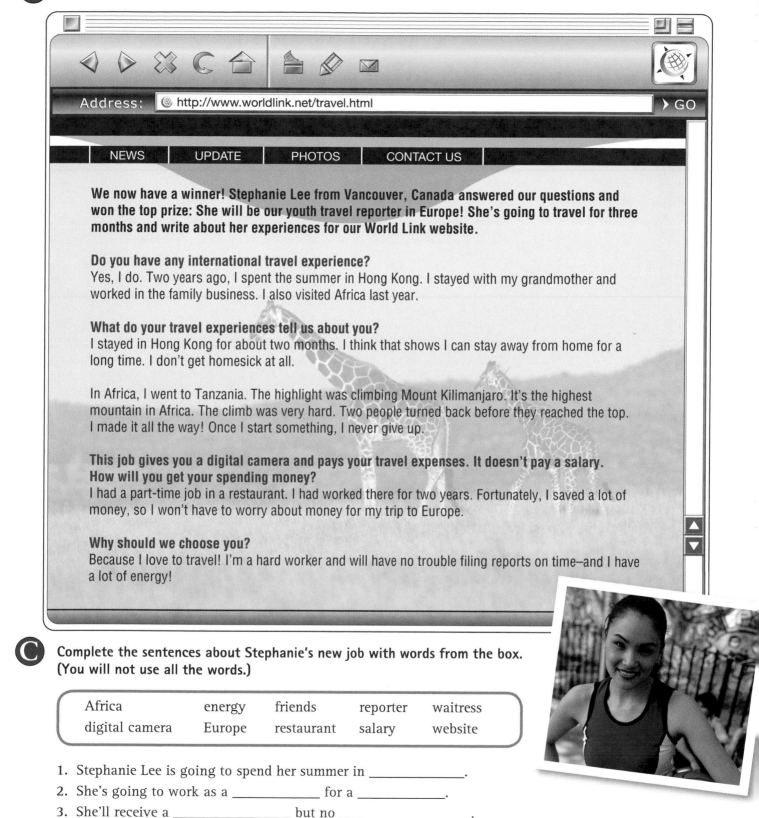

Address: http://www.worldlink.net/travel.html 〉GO

| NEWS | UPDATE | PHOTOS | CONTACT US |

We now have a winner! Stephanie Lee from Vancouver, Canada answered our questions and won the top prize: She will be our youth travel reporter in Europe! She's going to travel for three months and write about her experiences for our World Link website.

Do you have any international travel experience?
Yes, I do. Two years ago, I spent the summer in Hong Kong. I stayed with my grandmother and worked in the family business. I also visited Africa last year.

What do your travel experiences tell us about you?
I stayed in Hong Kong for about two months. I think that shows I can stay away from home for a long time. I don't get homesick at all.

In Africa, I went to Tanzania. The highlight was climbing Mount Kilimanjaro. It's the highest mountain in Africa. The climb was very hard. Two people turned back before they reached the top. I made it all the way! Once I start something, I never give up.

This job gives you a digital camera and pays your travel expenses. It doesn't pay a salary. How will you get your spending money?
I had a part-time job in a restaurant. I had worked there for two years. Fortunately, I saved a lot of money, so I won't have to worry about money for my trip to Europe.

Why should we choose you?
Because I love to travel! I'm a hard worker and will have no trouble filing reports on time—and I have a lot of energy!

C Complete the sentences about Stephanie's new job with words from the box. (You will not use all the words.)

| Africa | energy | friends | reporter | waitress |
| digital camera | Europe | restaurant | salary | website |

1. Stephanie Lee is going to spend her summer in _____.
2. She's going to work as a _____ for a _____.
3. She'll receive a _____ but no _____.
4. Stephanie is perfect for the job because she has a lot of _____.

ask**&**
ANSWER
Would you like to do Stephanie's job? Why or why not? Tell about a summer job that you have had.

Predictions with *be going to* and *will*

A People use *be going to* and *will* to make predictions (guesses about the future).
Look at the pictures and read the captions. Then fill in each blank below with *be going to* or *will*.

"Look! That truck **is going to** go through that red light!"

"He's **going to** be successful in his new job." *or*
"He'll be successful in his new job."

1. In picture A, we can see that the action is happening now or very soon, so we use _____ but not _____.

2. In picture B, we are talking about a more distant time in the future, so we use _____ or _____.

B Look at the chart. It shows the different uses of *be going to* and *will*.
Complete the sentences with *be going to*, *will* or both plus the verb in parentheses.

	a decision made in the past	a sudden decision	an action happening soon	an action happening in the more distant future
be going to	✓		✓	✓
will		✓		✓

1. Next year he _____is going to go / will go_____ to boarding school. (go)
2. She's getting bigger and bigger. She _____ a baby soon. (have)
3. The phone is ringing. I _____ it. (answer)
4. I bought my ticket last month. I _____ in Europe this summer. (travel)
5. I need money right now. I think I _____ some. (borrow)
6. She was accepted to two colleges. She _____ Stanford. (attend)
7. Look at those dark clouds. It _____ soon. (rain)

C Pair work. Compare your answers in B with a partner's.
Explain why you chose *be going to*, *will*, or both.

5 Writing

My life now and in the future

 A Use the topics below or ones of your own. First write about what you are doing now. Then write about your future. Use *be going to* and *will* to make predictions.

> family　job　travel　school　love life

> **My Life Now and in the Future**
> Right now, I'm taking an English class.
> I'm working part-time at a video store.
> I live at home with my parents and two
> brothers. I have a boyfriend.
> Someday, I'm going to get married and
> live in a house by the ocean. Sooner or
> later, I'll . . .

B Pair work. Exchange papers with a partner. Do you think your partner's predictions will come true?

6 Communication

Predicting the future

A Read this profile of Prince William.
With a partner, make some predictions about his future.

Birthday:	June 21, 1982
Schooling:	He went to Eton College near Windsor. Then he went to the University of St. Andrews in Scotland. He studied art history.
Hobbies:	He loves sports, including rugby, hockey, swimming, skiing, and running. He likes to listen to music.
Personality:	He is shy in public. In private, he is strong-willed and independent. He is mature for his age.

> *He's going to serve in the Royal Navy. His father did.*

> *I think he'll marry someone famous, like a movie star.*

B Now complete your own personal profile.

Schooling:	
Hobbies:	
Personality:	

C Pair work. Exchange profiles with a partner.
Make predictions about your partner.

> *I think you are going to succeed in business. And you'll . . .*

 Check out the World Link video.　　 **Practice your English online at** <u>worldlink.heinle.com.</u>

1 Storyboard

A Ruben is shopping in the supermarket. Complete the conversations. For some blanks, more than one answer is possible.

B Pair work. Practice the conversations. Then change roles and practice again.

C Pair work. Role play. Make your own conversation. Use the word *vegetarian (made without meat or fish)* in your conversation. Then act out the conversation.

2 See it and say it

A Look at the pictures. Answer the questions.

1. Who is Madame Zorba? What is she doing?
2. Why are these people visiting her?

Madame Zorba

OCTOBER 16

In the future, you . . .

③ Anita

OCTOBER 18

CONGRATULATIONS! SCHOLARSHIP

I have no self-confidence.

④ Javier

I love my new sports car!

I'm lonely.

OCTOBER 26

① Cindy

⑤ EXIT Brian

Our supervisor isn't very nice.

I'm unemployed.

OCTOBER 17

② Tom

B Pair work. On October 16th, Madame Zorba made five predictions. You can see her predictions in the pictures above. With your partner, make sentences to express her predictions. Use the time expressions in the box.

in the future	sooner or later	the day after tomorrow
tomorrow	one of these days	the week after next

Tom is unemployed now, but tomorrow he'll find a good job.

C Pair work. What should the people do now? Think of advice for them.

D Pair work. Write down three statements about your life now. Exchange papers with a partner. Take turns making predictions and giving advice to your partner.

Review: Units 4-6 **67**

3 I don't understand this machine.

A Pair work. Use the verbs in the box to fill in the blanks in the scrambled conversation below. (You will use some words more than once.)

> add   put   set   wait

1. B: It's easy. First, _____ everything in the machine.
   Then _____ the temperature dial.
2. A: Excuse me. Do you work here?
3. B: Good. _____ your money in the machine.
4. A: Thanks for your help!
5. B: Two dollars. Do you have change?
6. B: Yes, I do. How can I help you?
7. B: _____ for the light to come on.
   Then _____ the detergent.
8. A: Yes, I do. I brought a lot of quarters.
9. A: Well, I don't understand this machine.
10. A: Let's see . . . I think "cold" is best. Now, how much does it cost?
11. A: OK, I've put the money in. Here's my last question. When do I _____ the detergent?

B Pair work. Now put the sentences in order to make a conversation.

The correct order is __2,_____

C Pair work. Role play. Choose a process below. Ask your partner about the process.

bake a birthday cake   send an e-mail message   use a friend's cell phone

> *How do you bake a birthday cake?*

> *It's easy. First, read the recipe and get everything ready. Then, . . .*

4 Listening: Sure, no problem.

Check (✓) the best response to each sentence you hear. (CD 1, Track 43)

1. ☐ Sure, no problem.
   ☐ No, not at all.
2. ☐ Can I help you?
   ☐ OK. Go right ahead.
3. ☐ You ought to stay indoors. Do something fun.
   ☐ You shouldn't stay indoors. Do something fun.
4. ☐ Yes, not at all.
   ☐ No, not at all.

5. ☐ Look! It's going to fall!
   ☐ Look! It will fall!
6. ☐ You had better turn right.
   ☐ Turn right at the signal.
7. ☐ OK. I'll take two tickets for the 4:00 show.
   ☐ OK. I'm going to take two tickets for the 4:00 show.
8. ☐ You should buy the green one.
   ☐ You had better buy a sweater.

5 My list of errands

A Pair work. Role play. Choose one of the four errands below. Get the person's attention. Then ask and answer at least two more questions.

1. **At the garage**

    Customer: Your car needs to be repaired.

    Mechanic: Your schedule is very tight.

2. **On campus**

    Student: You need to register for a class. It meets on Mondays.

    Advisor: There is only one English class open on Tuesday night.

3. **At the campus health center**

    Patient: You need to get a flu shot.

    Clerk: There aren't any appointments available this week.

4. **At a gift shop**

    Customer: You found a birthday present for a friend. You want to buy it and have it wrapped.

    Clerk: You are very busy.

B Pair work. Role play. Choose another situation and change roles.

Excuse me, do you work here?

Yes, I do. Can I help you?

There's a problem with my car . . .

6 Word relationships

Use the words in the box to complete the expressions below.

> hall   estate   center   paper   service   half
> roll   ~~school~~   rise   list   made

1. boarding _school_
2. day care _____
3. errand _____
4. grocery _____
5. high _____
6. honor _____
7. one _____
8. real _____
9. study _____
10. tailor-_____
11. term _____

7 Listening: Current statistics

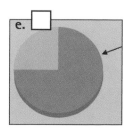

Listen to each statistic. Write the number you hear on the picture it describes. (CD 1, Track 44)

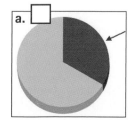

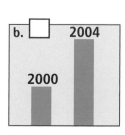

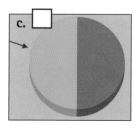

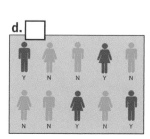

1 Vehabulary Link

Different kinds of parties

A Look at these pictures of parties. Then take the quiz below.

baby shower

bachelor party

block party

housewarming party

barbecue

family reunion

slumber party

surprise party

American party quiz

1. You hold a **baby shower** before / after a baby is born.
2. A **bachelor party** is for a woman / man before he / she gets married.
3. People at a **block party** live near each other / work together.
4. At a **housewarming party,** you usually receive gifts / money for your new home.
5. A **barbecue** is usually held after it snows / on a warm, sunny day.
6. A **family reunion** is for your immediate family only / your family and relatives.
7. When kids go to a **slumber party,** they stay overnight / eat dinner and go home.
8. An important thing to do before a **surprise party** is spend a lot of money / keep a secret.

B Pair work. Compare your answers with a partner's.

ask**&**
ANSWER
Which parties are familiar to you? Which ones are unfamiliar? Which parties would you like to attend?

2 Listening

A catering company

 A Listen. Jared is going to work for a catering company.
What does a catering company do? Check *a*, *b*, or *c*. (CD 2, Track 1)

A catering company . . .

☐ **a.** produces and plays music.

☐ **b.** prepares and serves food.

☐ **c.** makes and sells clothing.

 B Listen again. What will Jared do in his job? Circle the correct answers. (CD 2, Track 2)

1. before the party
   a. cook food
   b. set up
   c. call the guests

2. during the party
   a. serve food and drinks
   b. collect money
   c. watch the food

3. after the party
   a. say "thank you"
   b. wash dishes
   c. put things in the truck

ask & ANSWER

Would you like to work for a catering company? Would you ever hire a catering company for a party? Why or why not?

3 Pronunciation

Reduced *want to* and *would you*

  A Listen to the sentences. Notice the reduced pronunciation of the underlined words. Then listen again and repeat. (CD 2, Track 3)

1. Do you <u>want to</u> go hiking?
2. Do you <u>want to</u> have dinner?
3. <u>Would you</u> like to go hiking?
4. <u>Would you</u> like to have dinner?

  B Listen and circle the words you hear. (CD 2, Track 4)

1. Do you want to / Would you like to go to a concert?
2. Do you want to / Would you like to see a movie?
3. Do you want to / Would you like to study together?
4. Do you want to / Would you like to come to my birthday party?

 C Pair work. Use the sentences in A or B to invite your partner to do different things. Make plans.

Do you want to go hiking?   I'd love to!

Speaking

It's a pool party.

 A Listen to the conversation. Does Lane accept or refuse Omar's invitation? (CD 2, Track 5)

Omar: Did you hear the news? Sayuri is having a party.

Lane: Really? When?

Omar: On Wednesday. It's a pool party.

Lane: Cool! That sounds like fun.

Omar: Do you want to go with me?

Lane: But I don't know Sayuri.

Omar: No problem. She said I could bring a friend.

Lane: Well, OK. I'd love to go. What time is the party?

Omar: It starts at 3:00. Why don't we meet at my house at 2:30?

Lane: Sounds good!

 B Pair work. Practice the conversation with a partner.

ask & ANSWER

Would you enjoy a pool party? Why or why not?
Talk about the last party you went to. Was it fun?

5 **Speaking Strategy** 🔧

Accepting and refusing invitations

 A What do you like to do in your free time?
Check the boxes. Then add four more things to the list.

☐ see a movie	☐ study English
☐ go swimming	☐ go shopping
✓ _____	✓ _____
✓ _____	✓ _____

B Pair work. Invite each other to do the activities in A.
Accept or refuse your partner's invitations.

Useful Expressions:	
Accepting invitations	**Refusing invitations**
Sure!	I'm sorry, but I can't.
That sounds great!	Unfortunately, I can't.
I'd love to!	I'd love to, but I'm busy.

Do you want to go to the zoo this afternoon?

I'm sorry, but I can't. I have to work. How about tomorrow?

6 Language Link

Inviting using infinitives and the *-ing* form

 A Study the chart.

Expressions for making invitations

Expressions followed by the infinitive	Expression followed by the *-ing* form
Do you want How would you like to go with me? Would you like	Would you be interested in going with me?

 B Pair work. Practice the conversation with a partner. Then make new conversations using the expressions in the box. Accept or refuse the invitations.

A: Would you be interested in having dinner on Friday?
B: Sure. What time?
A: Do you want to meet at 8:00?
B: OK!

Expressions
1. How would you like . . . Would you be interested in . . . Would you like . . .
2. go to a block party come over for dinner see a movie
3. this afternoon Saturday night tomorrow

C Pair work. Invite your partner to one of the events below. Then switch roles.

Weekend Events

12-hour dance-athon!
Come and dance the day away!
Friday, December 17
Doors open: 12 noon / $25
All profits go to charity.

Comedy night at The Café—join us!
See your favorite comedians on our stage!
Friday, December 17
9:00 p.m. / $15
Popcorn and soda will be provided.

Concert
City Orchestra plays your holiday favorites!
7:00 p.m. / $7
Friday, December 17
The program will run approximately 1 hour.

Art gallery event—free viewing
New show opening tonight!
Friday, December 17
Party starts at 5:00 p.m.
Come and support your local artists.

Party planning

 A Pair work. You are planning a party. Choose an item from each category or think of an item of your own.

TYPE OF FOOD

a. finger foods

b. barbecue

c. burger and fries   d. pasta and salad

PLACE

a. a friend's house   b. a big warehouse

c. a nightclub   d. a park

TYPE OF PARTY

a. masquerade party

b. reunion party

c. surprise party   d. dance party

PARTY THEME

a. western   b. luau   c. safari   d. sports

 B Class activity. Invite up to four other pairs to your party. Ask and answer questions about the parties.

Would you like to come to our party next week?

What kind of party is it?

It's a Hawaiian luau party. We're going to wear Hawaiian shirts and drink pineapple juice.

 C Pair work. Fill in the invitations you received from your classmates.

PARTY!

Food: _____

Place: _____

Type of party: _____

Theme: _____

PARTY!

Food: _____

Place: _____

Type of party: _____

Theme: _____

PARTY!

Food: _____

Place: _____

Type of party: _____

Theme: _____

PARTY!

Food: _____

Place: _____

Type of party: _____

Theme: _____

 D Pair work. Which party do you want to go to? Choose one with your partner and tell the class. Describe the food, place, type of party, and theme for the party.

Let's Celebrate!

Lesson B | Festivals and holidays

1 Vocabulary Link

Two festivals

A Look at the pictures of two festivals. Then read the sentences below and write *A* or *B*.

A.

B.

The Nebuta Festival

The Holi Festival

1. __A__ People rent a special **costume** called *haneto*. They wear the costume in the festival.
2. _____ Cities and towns **come alive** in India for this festival. It is very **colorful**.
3. _____ This festival takes place in August. It is a **well-known** festival in Japan.
4. _____ People **celebrate** by chasing and throwing colored powder on each other.
5. _____ There is a big **parade** at night with big, bright **floats**.
6. _____ A lot of **sightseers** come to see the big floats.
7. _____ Here's some **advice**: Wear a hat and sunglasses to protect yourself from all the powder!

B Think of a festival you know. Answer the questions about it. Then tell your partner about it.

1. What is the name of the festival? _____
2. When does it take place? _____
3. It is **well-known / not well-known**.
4. In this festival, you celebrate by _____
5. In this festival:
   ☐ you wear a costume   ☐ there are floats   ☐ other: _____
6. Here is a piece of advice for sightseers: _____

ask&
ANSWER

Would you prefer to participate in a festival or just watch? Why?
What is the most famous festival in your country?
What advice would you give a visitor to that festival?

2 Listening

Festival experiences

A Listen to Mark and Marissa talk about their experiences. Check (✓) the festival each one attended. (CD 2, Track 6)

	Nebuta	Holi
Mark	☐	☐
Marissa	☐	☐

B Listen again. Number the events (1 to 4) in each column in the order that they happened. (CD 2, Track 7)

1. Mark's experience

_____ danced in a parade

_____ watched floats on the river

_____ rented a costume

_____ injured his ankle

2. Marissa's experience

_____ mixed the powder with water

_____ sprayed a police officer

_____ received a water pistol

_____ bought colored powder

World Link

In Thailand, New Year's Day is celebrated from April 13th through the 15th. As part of the celebration, people throw water on each other!

3 Reading

Groundhog Day

What American holidays or festivals do you know?

A Groundhog Day is on February 2. Look quickly at the article. What do you think happens on that day? Check (✓) your answer.

a. ☐ People see a groundhog and make a wish.

b. ☐ People use a groundhog to predict the weather.

c. ☐ People have a big parade for the groundhog.

B Read the article about Groundhog Day.

The Chronicle

Pete Sees His Shadow Again!

Groundhog Day

A groundhog is a small animal covered with brown fur. It lives in a hole in the ground. During the winter, it stays underground and sleeps and eats. When people see the groundhog in the winter, they think spring is coming soon.

Punxsutawney Pete is a groundhog. He lives in Punxsutawney, Pennsylvania. On February 2, Pete's hometown comes alive—as many as 30,000 sightseers gather to celebrate Groundhog Day. Beginning in the morning, they watch for Pete to come out of his hole. Most years he comes out, sees his shadow, and runs back into the hole. That means there will be at least six more weeks of cold, wintery weather. Occasionally, Pete comes out of his hole and stays outside for a while. That's a good

sign. It means that spring weather will arrive soon.

After Pete appears, the people of Punxsutawney celebrate. There is a barbecue, a colorful festival in the park, a souvenir show and sale, and even a storytelling festival. There is a lot to do in this little town on Groundhog Day!

Pete is a famous groundhog. In 1986, he met the president of the United States. There was a big Hollywood movie made about him in 1993. And in 1995, he was a guest on the Oprah Winfrey show, a popular TV talk show.

Unfortunately, Pete has seen his shadow about 85 percent of the time since the tradition started in 1887. Let's hope next year is different!

 C Read these statements. Circle *True* or *False*.
Correct the false statements to make them true.

1. A groundhog is a large, black animal.	True	False
2. The town of Punxsutawney celebrates Groundhog Day.	True	False
3. Pete met the president of the United States.	True	False
4. A movie about Pete came out in 1995.	True	False
5. Pete doesn't usually see his shadow.	True	False

 D Pair work. Cover the reading and tell your partner what happens on Groundhog Day.

ask**&**
ANSWER

What late winter or early spring festivals do you know?
What happens in each one?

Time clauses with *before*, *after*, and *when*

A Each sentence in the chart below contains a time clause with *before*, *after*, or *when*. Notice the two ways of writing each sentence.

1a. We have dessert <u>after</u> we have dinner.

 b. <u>After</u> we have dinner, we have dessert.

(Both sentences tell us that first we have dinner, and then we have dessert.)

2a. <u>Before</u> the festival starts, we rent a costume.

 b. We rent a costume <u>before</u> the festival starts.

(Both sentences tell us that first we rent a costume, and then the festival starts.)

3a. <u>When</u> the groundhog comes out of his hole, everyone cheers.

 b. Everyone cheers <u>when</u> the groundhog comes out of his hole.

(Both sentences tell us that the groundhog comes out of his hole just an instant before everyone cheers.)

B Match a clause on the left with one on the right to make sentences about a typical day. Use each answer only once.

<u> b </u> 1. After I eat breakfast,

____ 2. Before I leave the house,

____ 3. I check my e-mail

____ 4. I have lunch

____ 5. I make my last phone calls

____ 6. When I get home from the office,

a. I take off my shoes and relax.

b. I brush my teeth.

c. I say "goodbye" to my cat.

d. after I work all morning.

e. after I turn on my computer.

f. before I leave the office.

C Pair work. Look at Paul's typical Christmas Day activities. Then, with a partner, combine different sentences using *before*, *after*, and *when*.

7:00 a.m. The alarm clock rings.	1:00 p.m. Everyone has lunch.
7:00 a.m. Paul gets up.	2:00 p.m. The adults talk and the children play games.
7:30 a.m. The family gathers in the living room.	5:00 p.m. The family drives home.
7:30 a.m. They open their presents.	6:00 p.m. They have Christmas dinner.
8:00 a.m. Everyone relaxes and enjoys the morning.	8:30 p.m. Everyone sings Christmas carols together.
12:30 p.m. The family drives to Grandmother and Grandfather's house.	10:00 p.m. Paul goes to bed.

When the alarm clock rings, Paul gets up.

5 Writing

In my country

 A Write about a festival or holiday you know.

B Pair work. Exchange papers with a partner.
Ask for more information about the holiday.

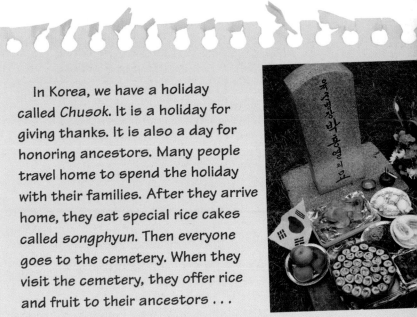

In Korea, we have a holiday called *Chusok*. It is a holiday for giving thanks. It is also a day for honoring ancestors. Many people travel home to spend the holiday with their families. After they arrive home, they eat special rice cakes called *songphyun*. Then everyone goes to the cemetery. When they visit the cemetery, they offer rice and fruit to their ancestors . . .

6 Communication

An unusual holiday

A Pair work. Look at these unusual holidays.
Then ask and answer the questions below with a partner.

National Ice Cream Day
July 20

World Hello Day
November 21

World Tourism Day
September 27

National Men Make Dinner Day
November 7

1. What do you think happens on each day?
2. Which one(s) would you like to celebrate? Why?

B Pair work. Use the questions below to invent an unusual holiday.

- What is the name of the holiday?
- What is the date of the holiday?
- What is the reason for the holiday?
- Who celebrates it?

- What do people do on the holiday?
- Do people celebrate it at home or outside the home?
- What do people wear?
- Are there any special foods or decorations?

C Present your holiday to the class.

 Check out the World Link video.   **Practice your English online at** <u>worldlink.heinle.com</u>.

8 Fables and Fairy Tales

Lesson A | Animal tales

1 Vocabulary Link 🔁

Creatures of the great outdoors

A Look at the pictures.
Then match a word with a picture.

1. ant
2. fox
3. ~~grasshopper~~
4. lion
5. tortoise
6. crow
7. frog
8. hare
9. mouse

B Match each animal in A to the sentence that best describes it.
Write the number.

3	I'm small and I can jump high.		I'm black and I can fly.		I carry my house on my back.
	I'm small and I love cheese!		I'm green and I can hop.		I'm similar to a rabbit.
	I'm small and I work hard.		I'm clever and I look like a dog.		Another name for me is "King of the Jungle."

ask&
ANSWER

Which animal are you most afraid of?
Which is the smartest? Which is the strongest?

2 Listening

Four fables

 A Listen to these four fables. Write the number of each story in the box. (CD 2, Track 8)

 B Listen again. Circle *True* or *False*. (CD 2, Track 9)

1. The lion ate the mouse.   True   False
2. The tortoise won the race.   True   False
3. The grasshopper worked hard.   True   False
4. The fox ate the cheese.   True   False

 C Listen again. Match the title of each story to its main point. (CD 2, Track 10)

1. The Lion and the Mouse   a. Small friends are important, too.
2. The Tortoise and the Hare   b. It's best to prepare for the future.
3. The Ant and the Grasshopper   c. Slow and steady wins every time.
4. The Fox and the Crow   d. Be careful about kind words from a stranger.

ask**&** ANSWER   A *fable* is a story that teaches a lesson. Which fable did you like best? Why? Which main point in C do you think is most important? Why?

3 Pronunciation

Was vs. *wasn't*; *were* vs. *weren't*

 A Listen and check (✓) the sentence you hear. (CD 2, Track 11)

1. ☐ He was winning the race.   ☐ He wasn't winning the race.
2. ☐ She was walking to work.   ☐ She wasn't walking to work.
3. ☐ They were working hard.   ☐ They weren't working hard.
4. ☐ They were having fun.   ☐ They weren't having fun.

B Pair work. Read the sentences in A aloud. Practice with a partner.

C Pair work. Guess what your partner was doing yesterday at these times.

noon   5:00 p.m.   8:00 p.m.

4 Speaking

Not your typical fairy tale

  A Listen to the conversation. Did Zora like the movie? (CD 2, Track 12)

Chris: What were you doing last night around 7:00?

Zora: Last night? I was watching a movie. Why?

Chris: I tried to call you. You weren't home.
What movie did you see?

Zora: *Shrek*.

Chris: I don't know it.

Zora: It's an animated film. It was really good.

Chris: What's it about?

Zora: It's about a green monster named Shrek.
He rescues a princess named Fiona.

Chris: It sounds like a typical fairy tale.

Zora: Not exactly. The characters are really funny and the
story is surprising. You should see it!

 B Pair work. Practice the conversation with a partner.

ask&
ANSWER

Would you see a movie like *Shrek*? Why or why not?
Can you think of any other popular animated movies?

5 Speaking Strategy 🛠

Asking about movies

 A Think of a movie you like. Make some notes about it. Don't tell your partner the title!

Title: _____   Actors in the movie: _____

Setting: _____   _____

Plot: _____   _____

_____   _____

B Pair work. Your partner asks questions and guesses the movie title.

What's the movie about?

It's about a boy with magical powers.

Useful Expressions:
Asking about movies

What's the movie about?

What's the setting for the movie?

Who's in the movie?

What happens in the movie?

6 Language Link

The past continuous

A Read this short summary of part of the famous story, *The Lion King*.

Long ago, a great lion king named Mufasa was living in Africa. His evil brother, Scar, was supposed to be the next king. He was waiting for his next chance. Then Mufasa's son, Simba, was born, and everything changed. Simba was now next in line to become king. Scar became jealous of Simba. So he made a terrible plan to kill Mufasa and Simba. But only Mufasa was killed, and Simba escaped . . .

B Now read the following description of the past continuous.
Then underline the examples of the past continuous in the summary above.

The *past continuous* is formed as follows: *was/were* + verb + *-ing*
For example: *I didn't want to call him because he was studying.*

Stative verbs (for example, *be, seem, know, need*) are not normally used in the continuous form. Use the simple past with stative verbs.

> The past continuous is used to express a continuing action in the past.

C These statements were made the summer before Mufasa died.
Write the past continuous form of the verb, if possible. Watch for stative verbs.

1. The jungle ___was___ (be) beautiful, and everything _____ (seem) perfect. That summer was the happiest time of my life. I _____ (get) stronger and bigger as the days passed. My father _____ (train) me every day, and I _____ (dream) of becoming the king. I _____ (know) that I was the luckiest lion in the world.

2. I was the king of the lions. Everyone in the jungle was happy, except my brother, Scar. Every time I saw him, he _____ (talk) in secret with his friends. My young son, Simba, _____ (grow up) quickly, and I _____ (train) him to be the next king. Life was good, and everything in my kingdom _____ (go) well.

3. That summer _____ (seem) very strange and unpleasant to me, but I _____ (know) that soon my luck would change. You see, my friends and I _____ (plan) to get rid of my two biggest problems . . . forever. That little Simba _____ (grow up) too quickly. I _____ (need) to get rid of both of them before it was too late.

D Match each statement above with a character.

Mufasa

Simba

Scar

ask&
ANSWER

Do you know the rest of the story of *The Lion King*? Tell the rest of the story. If you don't know the story, how do you think the story probably ends?

7 Communication

A scrambled story

A Look at the pictures. Then put the parts of the story in order.

Please help me!

I'm going to eat you now.

Let's ask the hare!

The Clever Hare

a. ☐ The man believed the lion and helped him out of the hole. "Now, I'm going to eat you!" said the lion. "Help me! Help me!" yelled the man. Just then, a clever hare was hopping by.

b. ☐ Just then the lion realized his mistake. The man thanked the hare while the lion roared angrily from his hole. The man and the clever hare walked happily away.

c. ☐ "Please help me to get out of this hole!" said the lion. The man said, "But I'm afraid of you." The lion said, "Don't worry, I won't eat you!"

d. ☐ The man explained the situation to the clever hare. The hare thought quickly before he spoke.

e. ☐ Next the hare spoke to the lion. "You were in that deep hole before, right?" The lion growled, "Yes, I was." Then, without thinking, the lion jumped back into the hole.

f. 1 A man was walking in the forest on a beautiful, sunny day. He saw a lion in a deep hole.

g. ☐ "Before you eat me, let's ask that hare's opinion," said the terrified man. "OK, but ask quickly!" growled the lion.

h. ☐ First, the clever hare said, "Let me understand this clearly." The hare looked at the man and said, "You were standing over there before, right?" "Yes," said the man, and he went and stood beside the hole.

B Pair work. Compare your answers with a partner's. Discuss any differences.

C Pair work. Now retell the story to your partner in your own words.

ask **&**
ANSWER
What do you think this story teaches us?

Fables and Fairy Tales

Lesson B | Colorful characters

1 Vocabulary Link

Characteristics people have

A Look at the pictures. Then use the words to complete the sentences.

brave

loyal

compassionate

wise

disciplined

evil

determined

generous

1. Nothing can stop her from reaching her goal. She's very __determined__.
2. A _____ person is not afraid of anything.
3. She is kind to people and animals. She's _____.
4. A _____ person is always giving things to other people.
5. He's _____. He always supports the prince.
6. A _____ person is intelligent and gives good advice.
7. He's _____. He works very hard every day to support his family.
8. She is a bad person and wants to hurt people. She's _____.

B Discuss these questions.

1. What are the two most important characteristics for a best friend to have?
2. What characteristics are best for a parent to have?

2 Listening

What kind of person is she?

 A Listen to the three conversations. Then circle the correct answer to complete each sentence.
(CD 2, Track 13)

1. The boy isn't disciplined / kind.
2. Maria is compassionate / clever.
3. The boy is brave / generous.

 B Listen again. Choose two answers for each question. (CD 2, Track 14)

1. What did the boy do on the night before his test?

   a. saw a movie   b. study   c. ate ice cream

2. What does Maria do at the nursing home?

   a. clean   b. talk to people   c. serve meals

3. What did the boy give the girl?

   a. a pencil   b. a pen   c. some money

ask**&**
ANSWER

Are you disciplined? Explain your answer with an example.
Who are the kindest and most generous people you know?

3 Reading

The Cinderella story

 A Find the words in the reading that match the definitions.

1. treated in a cruel or unfair way (line 6) _____
2. a long dress worn on formal occasions (line 11) _____
3. differences (line 15) _____
4. ghost (line 16) _____
5. kindness (line 26) _____
6. wins (line 27) _____

World Link

The oldest Cinderella story is from China. It was written in 850 and is called "Yeh-shen." However, in this story, the slipper is golden.

The Cinderella story is a famous one. Cinderella was living happily with her family when her mother died. Her father remarried.
5 Cinderella's new stepmother and two stepsisters mistreated her. She was forced to wear old clothes and work hard while the sisters wore fancy clothes and had fun.

You know the rest of the story. A good witch
10 helped Cinderella. She turned Cinderella's old clothes into a beautiful gown. Cinderella went to a party and a prince fell in love with her. Cinderella left the party in a hurry and didn't tell the prince her name. But she did leave a glass slipper and the prince used that to find her. They got married and lived happily ever after.

15 The Cinderella story is found in many different countries with slight variations. In an African version, there is one stepsister, not two. In a version from the Philippines, a forest spirit helps the Cinderella character. Settareh, a Middle Eastern Cinderella, goes to a New Year's party.

Cinderella is not always a woman. In an Irish variation, a young boy, Becan, marries a princess and lives happily ever after. There's even a rap version of the story: Cinder-Elly wants to go to
20 a basketball game, not a party, to meet a basketball player.

Famous actresses have starred in the Cinderella story. Julie Andrews appeared in a 1957 TV version. More recently, the singers Whitney Houston and Brandy starred in another retelling of the story.

Why is the Cinderella story so popular? Why is the story found in so many cultures?
25 There are perhaps several reasons. First of all, it's a romantic story, which is a popular style. Also, Cinderella is a kind girl with a hard life. That makes people feel sympathy for her. Finally, she faces many challenges and triumphs in the end. The ending of the story makes everyone feel happy.

C Match the names on the left with the information on the right to make true sentences.

1. The African Cinderella   a. acted in a version of the Cinderella story.

2. Becan   b. attends a New Year's party.

3. Cinder-Elly   c. is a boy Cinderella.

4. The Philippine Cinderella d. goes to a basketball game.

5. Settareh   e. is helped by a forest spirit.

6. Whitney Houston   f. has only one stepsister.

ask **&**
ANSWER

Why do you think the Cinderella story is so popular?
Is there a Cinderella story in your country? If so, what is it?

4 Language Link

Past continuous vs. simple past

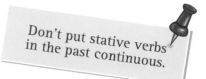
Don't put stative verbs in the past continuous.

A Look at the pictures and read the sentences. Then answer the questions below.

At noon, the hare (1) was running ahead.
At 2:00, the tortoise (2) finished the race first.

Cinderella (3) was crying when the good witch (4) appeared.

Which verb form above expresses . . .

☐ **a.** an action that is definitely finished?

☐ **b.** an action in progress at a certain time in the past?

Which verb form above expresses . . .

☐ **a.** a longer action?

☐ **b.** a shorter, interrupting action?

B Complete these sentences about a family and a frog with the verbs in parentheses. Use the simple past or the past continuous.

It **(1)** _____ (be) a beautiful day. The sun **(2)** _____ (shine) and

the birds **(3)** _____ (sing). A family **(4)** _____ (have) breakfast

when they **(5)** _____ (hear) a noise. Someone **(6)** _____ (knock)

at the door. The mother **(7)** _____ (open) the door. It **(8)** _____ (be)

a frog! The mother **(9)** _____ (scream). While the frog **(10)** _____ (hop)

away, the daughter **(11)** _____ (call) to him. The daughter **(12)** _____

(ask) the frog to stay. Because of her uncommon kindness, the frog **(13)** _____ (change)

into a handsome prince.

5 Writing

Fairy-tale diary

A Imagine you are a character in the Cinderella story. Write two or three entries in your diary from the point of view of your character. You can be the prince, a stepsister, the stepmother, or Cinderella.

B Pair work. Share your writing with a partner.

June 10: The party last night was wonderful. I danced with a mysterious girl. We were dancing, and then at midnight she suddenly ran out of the palace. Now I have a problem. I don't know her name. Maybe I should . . .

A Read the story.

Scene 1: (Characters: Jack and Jack's mother)
Jack lived with his mother. They were poor and owned only a cow. One day, the mother said to Jack, "We have no more food. Please go to the market and sell the cow."

Scene 2: (Characters: Jack and the magician)
On the way to the market, Jack met a magician. "I want to buy that cow," said the magician. "I will give you these magic beans for your cow." Jack was not very clever. He sold the cow for the beans!

Scene 3: (Characters: Jack and Jack's mother)
When Jack returned home, his mother was very angry. She threw the beans out the window. That night, the beans grew into a huge beanstalk. The next day, Jack climbed the beanstalk into the sky. He found a castle with a giant living in it. The giant owned a goose that laid golden eggs.

Scene 4: (Characters: Jack and the giant)
When the giant saw Jack he said, "I'm going to eat you." Jack said, "Let me cook you a big meal. It will be more delicious than me." The giant agreed. Jack cooked all day and night. The giant ate his meal and fell fast asleep.

 B Pair work. Your teacher will assign a scene to you and your partner. Create a conversation between the two characters in your scene. Perform your scene for the class.

Scene 5: (Characters: Jack and Jack's mother)
Jack quickly grabbed the goose, ran out of the castle, and climbed down the beanstalk. He chopped the beanstalk down so the giant couldn't follow him. Then he told the story to his mother. They lived happily ever after with the goose that laid golden eggs.

 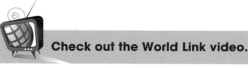

Check out the World Link video. **Practice your English online at** worldlink.heinle.com.

The World of Work

Lesson A | Work history

1 Vocabulary Link

Job qualities

A John works as a paramedic. Read what he says about his job.

- My job is for an active person—it's not a desk job.
- You should be careful with the patients, especially when you are moving someone who is injured.
- Some patients are polite and some are rude.
  You need to be pleasant with all the patients.
- A paramedic often works with no supervisor there, so it's important to be an independent worker.
- An emergency call can come at any time.
  A paramedic should be punctual when coming to work.
- Every day is different. You have to be flexible.

B Look again at the words in blue in A.
Write a word for each definition below.

1. nice to people _____
2. busy and energetic _____
3. on time _____

4. aware of danger _____
5. able to change easily _____
6. able to work alone _____

C Match the words on the left with their opposites on the right.

1. active   a. careless
2. careful   b. dependent
3. flexible   c. inactive
4. independent   d. inflexible
5. pleasant   e. late
6. punctual   f. unpleasant

ask & ANSWER

Complete this sentence: A paramedic should also be _____. Explain your answer.
Would you like to work as a paramedic? Why or why not?

2 Listening

What's the job?

 A Listen to three people talking about their jobs.
Write *Alice*, *Diane*, or *Mimi* under the appropriate picture. (CD 2, Track 15)

1. _____ 2. _____ 3. _____

 B Listen again. Change one word to make each false sentence true. (CD 2, Track 16)

1. a. Alice works ~~seven~~ days a week. _____six_____
   b. Alice gets good tips from her boss. _____
2. a. Diane is always late. _____
   b. Yesterday the lights went out. _____
3. a. Mimi's students are ten years old. _____
   b. The students have a lot of questions. _____

ask**&**
ANSWER

Which job would you like to have? Why?
Describe your ideal job.

World Link

The actor Bruce Lee was so fast, the studio slowed down the film so viewers could see his actions.

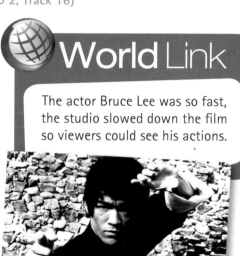

3 Pronunciation

Reduced *for* in time expressions

 A Listen to the sentences. Notice the reduced pronunciation of *for*. (CD 2, Track 17)

1. My father has worked there for decades.
2. I've lived in the same city for my entire life.
3. I've lived in this neighborhood for five years.

 B Listen to these sentences and write the time expression you hear. (CD 2, Track 18)

1. He's been sick _____.
2. I haven't eaten _____.
3. She's taught school _____.
4. I haven't seen him _____.

C Pair work. Complete the sentences with information about yourself.
Then say the sentences to a partner. Use reduced *for*.

1. I haven't been sick for _____.
2. I've lived in _____ for _____.
3. I've studied English for _____.

> I've lived in the same house for ten years.
> I've studied English for three years.

4 Speaking

What's new?

 A Greg and Juan are meeting for the first time since high school.
Listen to the conversation. How have they changed? (CD 2, Track 19)

Juan: Greg? Greg Anderson?
Greg: Juan Torres! How are you?
Juan: Great. How about you?
Greg: Just fine. What are you doing now?
Juan: Well, I just came back from Asia.
Greg: What were you doing there?

Juan: I was working in Osaka and studying Japanese.
Greg: Wow! Can you speak Japanese now?
Juan: Yes, I can . . . What's new with you?
Greg: Do you remember Kathy Morris?
Juan: Of course! She sat next to me in biology class.
Greg: Well, we got married. We've been married for two years now.

 B Pair work. Practice the conversation with a partner.

ask & ANSWER What things in your life have changed over the past few years?

5 Speaking Strategy

Asking about ability

 A Read about the skills needed for these popular jobs. Check (✓) the things you can do.

desktop publisher

- [ ] spell well
- [ ] design with a computer
- [ ] type for many hours
- [ ] follow detailed orders

personal home care assistant

- [ ] do household chores
- [ ] run errands
- [ ] listen patiently
- [ ] cook healthy meals

fitness instructor

- [ ] encourage others
- [ ] teach yoga
- [ ] train new members
- [ ] give advice on health

 B Pair work. Ask questions to find out which job your partner can do well. Use the Useful Expressions in the box.

Can you spell well? Are you able to type for many hours?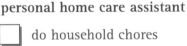

I can spell well, but I'm not very good at typing.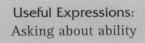

Useful Expressions:
Asking about ability

Can you spell well?
Are you able to type?
Are you good at cooking?
Do you know how to drive?

6 Language Link

The present perfect; *for* and *since*

 A Look at the time line and read the sentences below. Notice the verb forms in blue.

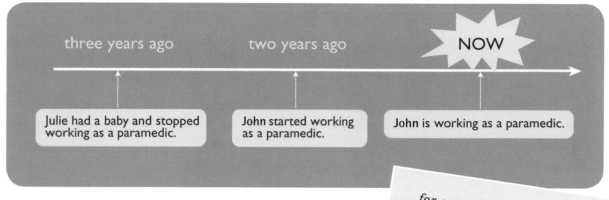

three years ago | two years ago | **NOW**

Julie had a baby and stopped working as a paramedic.

John started working as a paramedic.

John is working as a paramedic.

1. John has worked as a paramedic for two years.
2. Julie hasn't worked as a paramedic for three years.

for + a period of time: for three years
since + a point in time: since 2002
since + a past time clause: since I met him

B Complete the sentences. Circle the correct answers.

1. To form the present perfect, use the verb be / have + the past participle.
2. Use the present perfect for an action that started in the past / present.
3. Use the present perfect to show that an action was completed in the past / continues up to now.

C *For* and *since* are often used with the present perfect. Fill in the blanks with *for* or *since*.

1. _____ half an hour
2. _____ last year
3. _____ noon
4. _____ one month
5. _____ yesterday
6. _____ three hours
7. _____ we were children
8. _____ decades

D Complete these profiles. Use the present perfect with the verbs in parentheses and *for* or *since*.

"I _'ve lived___ (live) in the United States ____since___ August.
I _____ (study) English _____ I was in high school.
I'm studying for an exam right now. I _____ (not/sleep) well
_____ two days. I _____ (drink) three cups of coffee
_____ 9:00."

"He _____ (be) in college _____ three years.
He _____ (not/come) home _____ a year. I miss him.
He _____ (live) overseas _____ 2003.
We _____ (not/talk) on the phone _____ a month."

A Pair work. Work with a partner. Complete the job advertisements.
Use the qualities and abilities in the box below, and others of your own.

Qualities		Abilities	
good with children	kind to animals	able to walk long distances	able to build things quickly
good with tools	like computers	be a quick learner	have a high energy level

Metro Classifieds Your Guide to Great Jobs

DOG WALKER NEEDED.

Qualities needed: _____
_____
_____

Abilities needed: _____
_____

WORK AS A SUMMER CAMP COUNSELOR IN THE U.S.

Qualities needed: _____
_____

Abilities needed: _____
_____

WE'RE LOOKING FOR MOVIE SET DESIGNERS

Qualities needed: _____
_____

Abilities needed: _____
_____

WE NEED A WEB PAGE DESIGNER

Qualities needed: _____
_____

Abilities needed: _____
_____

B Role play. Choose a job in A to apply for. Your partner will interview you for the job using
the interview questions below.

Interview questions

1. What is your name?

2. Where do you work now?

3. How long have you worked there?

4. Are you _____?
   (quality)

5. Can you _____?
   (ability)

6. Do you know how to _____?
   (ability)

The World of Work

Lesson B | Dream jobs

1 Vocabulary Link

Two-word jobs

 A Pair work. Match the words in column A with the words in column B to make two-word jobs. Then write a two-word job below each picture.

A	B
1. farm	a. driver
2. fitness	b. hand
3. police	c. instructor
4. taxi	d. officer

A	B
5. fashion	e. attendant
6. film	f. designer
7. flight	g. director
8. tour	h. guide

a. _____

b. _____

c. _____

d. _____

e. _____

f. _____

g. _____

h. _____

B Pair work. Which person do you think made each statement?
Match each statement to a two-word job in A. Explain your answers.

1. "I think a lot about what's trendy." _____
2. "I know most of the addresses in this city." _____
3. "I'm outdoors a lot. I work with animals." _____
4. "I work with actors." _____

5. "I'm always flying to different cities." _____
6. "I know a lot about sightseeing." _____
7. "It's a dangerous job, but an important one." _____
8. "I think it's important to exercise." _____

 ask&
ANSWER

Which jobs would you like to try? Why? Which jobs wouldn't you like to do?

You need to move heavy objects sometimes.

 A Listen to Camille's job interview. Then answer the question. (CD 2, Track 20)

What job is she applying for?
a. flight attendant   **b.** fashion designer   **c.** tour guide

 B Listen again. Check (✓) *Yes* or *No* for each statement about Camille. (CD 2, Track 21)

	Yes	No
1. Camille graduated from college.	☐	☐
2. She speaks two foreign languages.	☐	☐
3. She has job experience.	☐	☐
4. She is physically fit.	☐	☐

3 Reading

I love my job!

What jobs are popular now among you and your friends?

A Read about Ken's and Steven's jobs on page 97. Then check (✓) *Ken* or *Steven* for each item in the box below.

	Ken	Steven
1. meets a lot of famous people	☐	☐
2. likes to drive	☐	☐
3. was on TV	☐	☐
4. crossed the desert	☐	☐

World Link

The world's largest employer is Indian Railways. It has more than 1,500,000 employees!

Source: *Guinness World Records, 2004*

B Read these job profiles. Then complete the summaries of Ken's and Steven's jobs below. Use the words in the box.

Ken

Steven

Interview 1

What is your job? I'm a V.J. or "video jockey."

How would you describe your job? I'm on TV. I introduce music videos and talk about them. I also interview singers who appear in videos.

What is the best part of your job? I get to meet a lot of famous people. That's very exciting. Also, I love music, so it's a lot of fun.

What is the worst part of your job? I get to meet a lot of famous people. Some of them are not very nice. They think they are better than me. They can be very demanding.

What was your most memorable moment? Last year, I presented an award on TV at a video music awards show. I couldn't believe it. They flew me out to Los Angeles and I stayed in Beverly Hills. I was on the TV show for a whole 45 seconds! I got to meet a lot of stars.

I want to be a V.J. How do I get the job? Well, first you have to make a videotape about yourself. You need to talk about certain things on the video. In my case, there was a list of questions, like "What did you do last weekend?" and "What's in your CD player right now?" After you talk about yourself, you send the videotape in to the TV station. They call you if they like the tape.

Interview 2

What is your job? I'm a car courier.

How would you describe your job? Sometimes a person or a company needs a car moved from one place to another. They hire me to drive the car. They may not have time to do it themselves.

What is the best part of your job? I like to drive, so it's fun for me. Last summer, I drove all the way from New York to California. The weather was great. I had the radio on and enjoyed my trip very much.

What is the worst part of your job? I have to be very punctual. If I say I'll arrive on Monday at 6:00, I have to be there by Monday at 6:00. I have to be dependable. It's stressful at times.

What was your most memorable moment? I drove across the desert as the sun was setting. It was incredible!

I want to be a car courier. How do I get the job? That's a good question. My mother started this business, so she hired me. You'd have to call my mother to find out!

drive	hired	interviews	loves	stressful
famous	independent	introduces	moves	videotape

Ken **(1)** _____ singers and **(2)** _____ music videos. He meets a lot of **(3)** _____ people. That's the good and the bad part of the job. He **(4)** _____ his job. He made a **(5)** _____ to get his job.

Steven **(6)** _____ cars from one place to another. He likes to **(7)** _____. You have to be **(8)** _____ to do his job and it can be **(9)** _____. Steven's mother **(10)** _____ him for the job.

ask**&**
ANSWER

Whose job would you like to have, Ken's or Steven's?
Think of a job you've had. What were the best and worst parts of that job?

4 Language Link

Verb + infinitive

A Study the chart.

These verbs can be followed by another verb in the infinitive form (*to* + verb):					
agree	choose	forget	learn	need	start
arrange	decide	hate	like	plan	try
attempt	expect	hope	love	prepare	want

B Which sentences have a verb in the infinitive? Circle the infinitive forms below. Not all the sentences have one.

1. They are planning (to move) to Mexico.
2. I chose to go to a large university.
3. I need a snack before I go to bed.
4. I like to buy presents for my friends.
5. I forgot the key to this door.
6. He hopes to meet her parents.
7. I expect him at ten minutes to three.
8. Do you want to work in an office?

C Complete the sentences below with the infinitive form of the verbs in the box.

go	help	open	~~speak~~	work

attend	become	graduate
perform	sing	work

Sanjay: I've always liked **(1)** __to speak__ foreign languages. I decided **(2)** _____ as an interpreter. I work at the United Nations.

Teresa: I chose **(3)** _____ to medical school because I wanted **(4)** _____ people. I'm planning **(5)** _____ a clinic in my hometown.

Dan: My sister is learning **(6)** _____. She wants **(7)** _____ in an opera someday.

Camille: I want **(8)** _____ a flight attendant. I need **(9)** _____ a six-week training course. I expect **(10)** _____ in August and start **(11)** _____ in September.

5 Writing

Writing about jobs

A Choose one of the topics below and write about it.

- a part-time or summer job you had
- a funny interview experience
- your dream job

B Pair work. Share your writing with a partner.

I like to swim. I decided to get a summer job as a lifeguard. There were many people trying to get the job.

I worked every day from 10:00 a.m. until 3.00 p.m.

A Group work. Get into groups of four: Students A, B, C, and D.
Get ready to play "Guess my job!" Read the instructions below.

taxi driver

flight attendant

rafting tour guide

ski instructor

film director

police officer

ranch hand

forest ranger

fashion designer

1. Student A secretly chooses one of the jobs above. Don't say the job you choose!

2. Students B, C, and D take turns asking one question each to discover Student A's job.
   Use a verb from the box below or one of your own.

try	choose	want	learn	need	plan
attempt	expect	hate	like	hope	love

3. After Student A answers the three questions, then together, Students B, C, and D take one guess
   to discover the job.

4. If the guess is incorrect, the game continues. Repeat steps 2 and 3 until someone guesses correctly.

 B Take turns being Student A, and play "Guess my job!" again.

 Check out the World Link video.   **Practice your English online at** <u>worldlink.heinle.com.</u>

1 Storyboard

A Harry is telling Linda about his dream. Complete the story. For some blanks, more than one answer is possible.

① I had a very strange dream last night.

Really? What _____?

② I _____ in the sky. It _____ very cold. In fact, it _____ .

I _____ lost. Then I _____ a farm. I _____ a farm hand.

We're having a party. Would you _____?

③

_____, but I can't. I'm in a hurry.

Suddenly I _____ a strange feeling . . . like I _____ into a hole.

Be careful!

④ Help!

Then I suddenly _____ . It _____ already morning.

⑤ 6:00

⑥ Wow! What do you think the dream means?

I have no idea!

B Pair work. Cover the story. Take turns telling the story to your partner.

C Pair work. Ask and answer these questions with a partner.

1. What do you think Harry's dream means?
2. Have you ever dreamed you were lost/flying/falling? Have you ever dreamed about animals?

2 See it and say it

A Pair work. Yesterday there was a movie premiere at the Galaxy Theater. Look at the picture. What were the people doing when the movie star arrived on the scene? Tell your partner.

B Pair work. Think of a movie you know. Write the name of the movie on the sign in the picture. Invite your partner to the premiere. Your partner should ask one or two questions.

Do you want to go to the premiere of Garden of the Gods?

I don't know. What's it about?...

C Class activity. Invite other friends to see the movie. Practice inviting and accepting or refusing invitations.

3 She's worked there for two years.

A Look at the pictures. Complete each person's job title.

 Ruth

 John

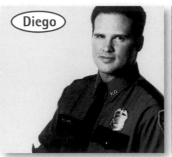 Diego

 Tonia

Web _____   _____ instructor   _____ officer   _____ driver

B Complete the sentences about each person in A.
Use the correct forms of the verbs in parentheses and circle *for* or *since*.

1. Ruth _____ (work) in the same company for / since two years.
   She _____ (hope/attend) graduate school next year.
2. John _____ (teach) exercise classes for / since the gym opened.
   He _____ (love/exercise)!
3. Diego _____ only _____ (have) this job for / since last Monday.
   He already _____ (want/find) a new job.
4. Tonia _____ (drive) a taxi for / since 2002.
   She _____ (plan/quit) soon.

4 Listening: A big party

 A Listen. Marcia and Dan are talking about party plans.
Circle the answer to each question. (CD 2, Track 22)

1. What kind of party is it?
   a. a barbecue   b. a baby shower   c. a surprise party
2. What is the relationship between Marcia and Dan?
   a. brother and sister   b. co-workers   c. best friends

 B Listen again. What is each person going to do? Write *D* for Dan or *M* for Marcia. (CD 2, Track 23)

1. _____ call the guests   3. _____ pick up cake.   5. _____ keep Mom and Dad
2. _____ meet Mom and Dad at 8:00   4. _____ put up decorations.   at restaurant.

5 Party planning

Group work. Follow the steps below. Plan a party.

- Decide what kind of party you're going to have.
- What tasks need to be done to prepare for the party? Make a list.
- Assign the tasks to your group members. Ask about ability.
- Tell the class about your party and preparations.

OK, we need a cake for our party.

Keiko, are you good at baking?

6 Amusing animals

 A Use the hints in parentheses to fill in the adjectives on the left and the animals on the right. Then read the six amusing animal names.

(giving things away)   ("February animal")

1. G __ N __ R __ __ S   G R __ __ __ __ H __ G

(faithful)   (animal in Africa)

2. L __ Y __ L   L __ __ __

(very busy)   (small insect)

3. A C __ __ V __   A __ __

(can change easily)   (lives in a pond)

4. F __ __ X __ __ L E   F __ __ __

(aware of danger)   (black bird)

5. C __ R __ F __ L   C __ __ __

B Pair work. Add an adjective before each animal name to make your own "amusing animals."

1. P_____   PIG
2. D_____   DOG
3. M_____   MONKEY

7 What kind of party is that?

 A Match columns A and B to make sentences about the parties below. Then write the number of each sentence next to a party.

Column A	Column B
1. Before the people walk in the door,	a. you see all your relatives.
2. After you heat up the grill,	b. they ask their parents for permission.
3. When you and your family go to this party,	c. everyone hides.
4. Before children can attend this party,	d. you take them a present for their home.
5. After this party is over,	e. you cook hamburgers and hot dogs.
6. When you visit a friend's new home,	f. it's nice to stay and help clean up the neighborhood.

☐ barbecue   ☐ housewarming party   ☐ slumber party

☐ block party   ☐ family reunion   [1] surprise party

B Think of a party you have gone to. What happened? Write four to six sentences on a separate piece of paper. Use time clauses.

I went to a party last weekend. It was really fun. Before the party started, . . .

C Pair work. Share your sentences with a partner. Ask and answer questions about your parties.

1 Vocabulary Link

A telephone quiz

A Match the words with the pictures.

1. answering machine
2. area code
3. (tele)phone directory
4. cell phone
5. cord
6. international call
7. local call
8. long-distance call
9. public (tele)phone
10. receiver
11. (tele)phone number

B Circle the best answer to complete each sentence.

1. A *pay phone* is another name for a _____.
   a. cell phone
   b. public telephone
2. The most expensive calls are usually _____ calls.
   a. local
   b. international
3. When the phone rings, you pick up the _____.
   a. receiver
   b. cord
4. Do you know the _____ for Boston?
   a. telephone number
   b. area code
5. I have more than twenty messages on my _____ today.
   a. answering machine
   b. telephone directory

ask & ANSWER

Do you like to talk on the telephone? Who do you call the most?
Do you ever make long-distance or international calls? Who do you call?

2 Listening

I need to make a phone call.

dial tone = the sound you hear when you pick up the phone

 A Listen. Who is making the telephone call in each situation? Check (✓) the name. (CD 2, Track 24)

	Mindy	Trey
Conversation 1	☐	☐

	Carla	Jerry
Conversation 2	☐	☐

 B Listen again. Circle the phrase that correctly completes each sentence. (CD 2, Track 25)

Conversation 1

1. At first, Trey is looking for a pay phone / his cell phone.
2. Mandy first tells Trey to press the send / power button.
3. Next, Mandy tells Trey to press the send / power button.

Conversation 2

1. At first, Carla tells Jerry to listen to the answering machine / look in the phone directory.
2. Then she tells him to call Maria / directory assistance.
3. Jerry is / isn't able to get Maria's phone number.

ask & ANSWER

Do you have an answering machine? What does the outgoing message say? Do you usually use a telephone directory? Why or why not?

3 Pronunciation

Repeating to clarify information

 A Listen to this conversation. Notice the intonation of B's sentence. Why does B stress the underlined number? (CD 2, Track 26)

A: My number is 555-6749.
B: 555-6<u>7</u>49?
A: Yes. 6-7-4-9.

 B Listen and complete the conversations. Then practice saying them aloud. (CD 2, Track 27)

1. A: My number is 555-2526.
   B: Did you say 555-_____?
   A: No, it's 2-5-2-6.

2. A: My work number is 800-555-5348.
   B: _____?
   A: That's correct.

3. A: You can call me back at 555-1661.
   B: Was that 555-_____?
   A: No, it's 1-6-6-1.

 C Pair work. Practice the conversations in B with a partner. Then use your own phone number and practice again.

4 Speaking

How do you spell that?

 A Yuka is calling Tony at his office. Listen to the conversation. (CD 2, Track 28)

Receptionist: Good morning. Barr Incorporated.

Yuka: Good morning. Tony White, please.

Receptionist: One moment, please.
I'm sorry. He's not in. May I take a message?

Yuka: Yes, please. Tell him that Yuka called.

Receptionist: Yuka. How do you spell that?

Yuka: It's spelled Y-U-K-A.

Receptionist: OK. Does Mr. White have your telephone number?

Yuka: Yes, he does.

Receptionist: OK, Yuka. I'll give him the message.

Yuka: Thanks a lot.

B Pair work. Practice the conversation. Imagine that you are calling Tony. Use your own name in the conversation.

ask&
ANSWER

Do you sometimes make telephone calls in English? Talk about your experiences. What is the hardest thing about telephoning in English?

5 Speaking Strategy

Spelling names

My name is Pablo. It's spelled P as in Papa, . . .

A Pair work. Use the chart on the right to practice spelling your name with a partner.

B Pair work. Role play. Imagine you are calling a friend at his or her office. Your partner role-plays the receptionist. Use the chart and Useful Expressions to help you.

Useful Expressions:	
Asking about spelling	Spelling
How do you spell that?	It's Y-U-K-A.
Could you spell that?	Sure. It's (spelled) Y-U-K-A.
	That's Y as in yellow . . .

A: Hello. Ms. Cabrini, please.
B: I'm sorry. She's not here. May I take a message?
A: Yes. Tell her Tad called.
B: Tad? Could you spell that, please?
A: Certainly. You spell it T as in tango, A as in apple, D as in Donald . . .

Words for spelling names

A - apple	N - Nancy
B - boy	O - orange
C - Charlie	P - Papa
D - Donald	Q - queen
E - England	R - Romeo
F - Frank	S - Susan
G - golf	T - tango
H - hot	U - uniform
I - island	V - Victor
J - Juliet	W - water
K - kilo	X - X-ray
L - love	Y - yellow
M - Mary	Z - zebra

6 Language Link

Modal expressions used on the telephone

 A When you speak on the telephone to someone you don't know, it is important to be polite. Practice saying the polite questions in the chart.

Polite questions	May I speak to Emi, please?	Could you call back later, please?
	Could you hold for a minute, please?	May I take a message?
	May I ask who's calling?	Would you like to leave a message?

 B Pair work. Silvio is talking to his girlfriend's roommate, Jen.
Make the conversation more polite. Write a question from the box in A on each line.

Jen: Hello?

Silvio: (1) <u>Is Emi there</u>?

1. _____

Jen: (2) <u>Who's this</u>?

2. _____

Silvio: Silvio.

Jen: (3) <u>Just a minute</u> . . . she's not here.

3. _____

(4a, 4b) <u>Is there a message</u>?

4. a. _____

Silvio: No . . . Will she be back soon?

   b. _____

Jen: She'll be home tonight.

(5) <u>You should call later</u>.

5. _____

C Pair work. Number the sentences to put them in order. Then practice with a partner.

Conversation 1
____ "It's Martin."
____ "Sure. May I ask who's calling?"
_1_ "Hello. May I speak to Kurt?"
____ "Can you hold for a minute, please?"

Conversation 2
____ "Otto? How do you spell that?"
_1_ "May I speak to Andy, please?"
____ "When will he be back?"
____ "Yes. Please tell him Otto called."
____ "It's spelled O-T-T-O."
____ "I'm sorry, but I don't know. Would you like to leave a message?"
____ "One moment please . . . I'm sorry, he's not here."

 World Link

Spell this one! *Hippopotomon-strosesquippedaliophobia* is one of the longest English words. It means "the fear of long words!"

Source: *Wikipedia*

Good news!

A Group work. Role play preparation. Get into groups of three: Student A, Student B, and Student C. Read the following instructions.

Student A: Choose one piece of good news from the list below.

| ☐ | Our friend had a baby! | ☐ | I got an "A" on my exam! |
| ☐ | I found your lost wallet! | ☐ | I got a new job! |

Student B: Have a piece of paper and a pen ready to write down a message.

Student C: Choose a reason you are busy from the list below.

| ☐ | You're taking a nap. | ☐ | You're out with friends. |
| ☐ | You're at the library. | | |

B Group work. Role play. Role-play these three conversations.

Step 1: Student A wants to give some good news to Student C, but Student B answers the phone. Student B explains why Student C is busy and takes Student A's message.

> A: Hello. May I speak to Bianca, please?
> B: I'm sorry, she's taking a nap. May I take a message?
> A: Yes. This is Ernesto. Please tell her to call me back. I have some good news.
> B: OK. What's your telephone number?
> A: It's . . .

Step 2: Student B writes down the message and gives the information to Student C.

> ● **:: WHILE YOU WERE OUT ::** ●
> Ernesto **called.**
> **Time:** 12:30
> **Message:** Please call him back.
> **Phone number:** 555-9733

Step 3: Student C calls Student A back to find out about the good news.

> C: Hi, Ernesto. It's Bianca.
> A: Hi, Bianca. I have some good news. Our friend had a baby!
> C: That's great! Is it a boy or a girl?
> A: It's a boy.
> C: When was he born? . . .

C Group work. Switch roles so everyone gets a chance to play each role.

Telecommunications

Lesson B | Crazy for cell phones

1 Vocabulary Link

Using the phone

 A In each item below, there are two verbs that are often used with the noun phrase on the right and one that is not. Cross out the verb that is not normally used with the noun phrase.

	Verbs		Noun phrases
1. enter*	try	~~answer~~	a phone number
2. leave	make	take	a message
3. speak to	answer	hang up	a phone
4. make	receive	try	a phone call
5. call	make	dial	a wrong number
6. pay	receive	answer	a phone bill
7. pick up	put down	dial	a receiver
8. get	try	hear	a busy signal

* for cell phones

B Pair work. Write your answers to the questions. Then interview your partner. Compare your answers.

1. What do you say when you leave a message?
   Me: _____
   My partner: _____

2. Who usually answers the phone in your home?
   Me: _____
   My partner: _____

3. Who makes the most phone calls in your family?
   Me: _____
   My partner: _____

4. What do you say when you call a wrong number?
   Me: _____
   My partner: _____

5. How much is your phone bill every month?
   Me: _____
   My partner: _____

 ask & ANSWER

Have you ever left a message in English?
What did you say?
Do you ever let the answering machine pick up a call even when you're at home?
Why or why not?

World Link

There are more telephones in Washington, D.C. than there are people!

Source: *Hooked on Facts*

2 Listening

I'll try again later.

 A Listen to Dave and Elaine trying to reach Henry by phone.
Check (✓) *yes* if the caller reaches him. Check (✓) *no* if the caller doesn't.
(CD 2, Track 29)

Conversation 1	☐ yes	☐ no
Conversation 2	☐ yes	☐ no

 B Listen again. Number the steps in the order that they happen. (CD 2, Track 30)

Conversation 1
_____ Elaine gives Dave a phone number.
_____ Dave gets a busy signal.
_____ Dave gets a voice mail system.
_____ Dave calls a cell phone number.

Conversation 2
_____ Elaine reaches Henry.
_____ Elaine talks to a little boy.
_____ Elaine dials a wrong number.
_____ Elaine calls again.

ask**&**
ANSWER
Do you know a person whose telephone is always busy?
Is yours always busy?

3 Reading

Cell phone usage

What kinds of calls do people use cell phones for?

A Read these statements. Check (✓) the ones that best describe you.

☐ I'm addicted to my cell phone. I use it all the time! ☐ I don't own a cell phone and don't want one.

☐ I think cell phones are very convenient. ☐ I think cell phones are great time savers.

☐ I only use a cell phone when I have to. ☐ Cell phones are annoying and unnecessary.

B Circle *T* for true or *F* for false after reading the article on page 111 about cell phone usage.

1. A majority of people think cell phones are unnecessary.   T   F
2. Phil is addicted to his cell phone.   T   F
3. Sherry probably uses her cell phone at special times.   T   F
4. Eric likes cell phones.   T   F
5. Carmen thinks cell phones save time and money.   T   F
6. Cities are passing laws about cell phone usage.   T   F

THE DAILY SUN

How do you feel about cell phones?

It can't be denied: there has been a cell phone boom in the last decade. Everywhere you go, people seem to be talking on the telephone. How do people feel about cell phones? Our on-the-street survey found some interesting answers.

Sixty-nine percent of the people we asked think cell phones are convenient and save time. Nineteen percent use cell phones only when they have to. A small percentage—only three percent—think cell phones are unnecessary. Another three percent say they are addicted to their cell phones!

There have been some problems associated with cell phones. Some cities have passed laws affecting cell phone use. For example, in some places, it is now illegal to drive and use your cell phone at the same time. A survey asked people about cell phones and laws. Here is how they answered:

There should be laws about cell phone usage…
    in classrooms, theaters, and restaurants.   57% agree
    while driving.   45% agree
    on public transportation.   34% agree

One thing is sure about cell phones: everyone has an opinion about how and when they should be used!

Read what these four people had to say:

I love talking on the phone. I keep my phone next to my bed. I even take it with me into the bathroom! My friends say that I am "cell phone crazy." – Phil

Cell phones are unnecessary. Why do people use them so often, especially in public places? I think it's a form of noise pollution! – Eric

I live in the country. My nearest neighbor is 25 miles away. My cell phone makes me feel safe. I can call someone in an emergency. – Sherry

I'm very busy. Sometimes I have to cancel an appointment at the last minute. I use my cell phone to do that. It's good for business. – Carmen

---

ask**&**
ANSWER

Would you ever take or make a cell phone call in a classroom? while driving? in a theater? on public transportation? in a restaurant? Look at the statistics in the reading. Do you think there should be laws about cell phone usage? Give reasons for your opinion.

4 Language Link

Verb + gerund vs. verb + infinitive

A gerund is the base form of a verb + *ing*.

A Study the chart.

Verbs followed by infinitive only		Verbs followed by gerund only		Verbs followed by gerund or infinitive	
agree	plan	appreciate	feel like	can't stand	prefer
choose	prepare	avoid	finish	continue	start
decide	seem	can't help	imagine	like	try
hope	want	dislike	keep	love	
learn	would like	enjoy	suggest		
need		(not) mind			

B Notice the use of the gerund or the infinitive in each sentence. Check (✓) the sentences that are correct.

1. ☐ I learned to speak Spanish when I was four.

2. ☐ I avoid to use cell phones in public places.

3. ☐ I like playing sports.

4. ☐ I appreciated to receive such a beautiful gift.

5. ☐ I agreed turning off the ringer on my phone.

6. ☐ I prefer to leave now.

C How do you feel about these activities? Use the verbs in the box with the phrases in parentheses to write sentences.

avoid	dislike	hate	love	need
can't stand	enjoy	like	(not) mind	want

1. (work on weekends) _I need to work on weekends._
2. (talk on the phone) _____
3. (get wrong numbers) _____
4. (eat junk food) _____
5. (cook at home) _____
6. (go to the beach) _____
7. (study) _____
8. (spend time outdoors) _____

D Pair work. Show your sentences to a partner. Compare your feelings about the different activities.

> I like to talk on the phone.

> Really? Not me. I avoid talking on the phone.

5 Writing

Opinions about cell phones

A Write about one of these topics or a topic of your own.

- People should avoid using cell phones while driving.
- I take my cell phone everywhere.

B Pair work. Exchange papers with a partner. Compare and discuss your feelings about cell phones.

> People should avoid talking on their cell phones while driving. I like to talk on the cell phone, but not while I'm driving. It's too dangerous! When you make a phone call in your car, you are not paying attention to the road.

6 Communication

How young is too young?

Do you think young children should have cell phones? Why or why not?

 A Pair work. Take this quiz about children and cell phones.
Compare your answers with a partner. Then check your answers on page 154.

Cell Phone Quiz

1. A survey in the U.S. says ___ of 8 to 12 year olds have a cell phone.

a. 4%

b. 21%

c. 45%

2. A study in Britain says that cell phones may be dangerous for children's ___.

a. brains

b. ears

c. voices

3. A recent law in Bangladesh says that children under 16 cannot ___ cell phones.

a. buy

b. sell

c. use

4. In Japan, more than 80% of teenagers and ___ of junior high school students have cell phones.

a. 5%

b. 25%

c. 60%

B Evan is twelve years old. He wants a cell phone. Read what each person thinks about the situation.

Evan Logan

Mrs. Logan

Mr. Logan

Evan's doctor

"I want to get a cell phone. All my friends have one. I need one to make phone calls and play games."

"I can't relax unless Evan has a phone. I want to be able to reach Evan immediately if I have to."

"Why does a 12-year old need a cell phone? He's a kid! He should be playing, not making phone calls."

"Cell phones are convenient, but it may not be safe for children to use them a lot."

 C Group work. Role play. Get into groups of four. Each student role-plays a person in B. Discuss whether Evan should get a cell phone.

Dad, I want to get a cell phone. All my friends have one!

Evan, you don't need to have a cell phone. I think you should wait until you're sixteen to get one.

 Check out the World Link video.

 Practice your English online at worldlink.heinle.com.

Technology Today

Lesson A | Computers are everywhere.

1 Vlcabulary Link

Computer words

A Many common English words have different meanings when they are used to talk about computers. Look at the pictures and study the words.

mouse

icon

menu

window

address

crash

surf

hardware

B Use the correct forms of the words in A to complete the sentences. Use each word twice.

Common usage

1. Could you open the __window__? It's hot in here.
2. My _____ is 223 Oak Street.
3. I went to the _____ store to buy a hammer.
4. The _____ ran into its hole.
5. I'm hungry, but I don't see anything I like on the _____.
6. Marilyn Monroe is a movie _____ from the 1950s.
7. When I was in California, I went _____ every day.
8. He accidentally _____ his car into a tree.

Computer usage

9. My computer _____. Can you fix it?
10. Plug the _____ into the keyboard.
11. He is always _____ the net for the latest news.
12. Open the other web page in a new __window__.
13. An _____ is a small picture on a computer screen.
14. The _____ is the machinery inside a computer.
15. First, click on an item in the _____.
16. Do you know her e-mail _____?

2 Listening

Computer problems

 A Listen to some people talk about different situations with their computers. Match each situation and its problem. (CD 2, Track 31)

Situation 1   **a.** a problem with a keyboard

Situation 2   **b.** an e-mail problem

Situation 3   **c.** a hardware problem

 B Listen again. Circle the correct word. (CD 2, Track 32)

1. The man was e-mailing his mother / friend.
2. The man clicked on Reply to Sender / to All.
3. The woman received a new computer / keyboard.

4. The woman spilled soda / coffee.
5. The man thinks the woman needs a new computer / mouse.
6. The woman's computer is five / ten years old.

ask & ANSWER

How would you fix a computer problem? Would you ask a friend for help? call a repair service? look for the answer in a manual?

World Link

The computer technology used in a Game Boy in 2000 was more powerful than the technology used to put the first man on the moon.

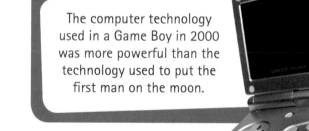

3 Pronunciation

Pronunciation of *s* in *used to* and *use/used*

 A Listen to the sentences. Notice the different pronunciation of the *s* in *used to* and the *s* in the verb forms *use* or *used*. (CD 2, Track 33)

used to/didn't use to: s = /s/	*use/used: s = /z/*
1. I used to type my term papers on a typewriter.	3. What kind of computer do you use?
2. I didn't use to wear scarves.	4. I used my brother's cell phone.

 B Listen for the pronunciation if *s* in the underlined words. Check (✓) /s/ or /z/. (CD 2, Track 34)

	/s/	/z/
1. She <u>used</u> the phone in her office.	☐	☐
2. He <u>used</u> to paint his own house.	☐	☐
3. Do you <u>use</u> a computer?	☐	☐
4. I didn't <u>use</u> to eat meat.	☐	☐

C Pair work. Take turns reading the sentences in B aloud with a partner.

4 Speaking

We used to write our papers on typewriters.

 A Listen. Steve is helping his daughter, Lea, with her term paper. How did Steve use to write his papers? (CD 2, Track 35)

Lea: I hate writing term papers! It takes forever!

Steve: You're lucky, Lea. When I was young . . .

Lea: Oh, I've heard this story before.

Steve: Well, when I was young, we didn't have computers. We used to write our papers on typewriters.

Lea: Oh, really? That sounds difficult!

Steve: It was, especially because I made a lot of mistakes.

Lea: Did it take a long time?

Steve: Yes. Computers are so much faster and easier to use.

 B Pair work. Practice the conversation with a partner.

ask**&**
ANSWER
Do you think that personal computers make our lives better? Why or why not?

5 Speaking Strategy

Showing interest

 A Complete these sentences with your own information.

1. In my spare time, I sometimes _____.
2. I'm afraid of _____.
3. I live in _____, but I would like to move to _____.
4. My favorite singer/movie/magazine is _____.

 B Pair work. Student A shares a personal fact from A. Student B shows interest and asks a follow-up question. Then switch roles.

In my spare time, I sometimes write short stories.

That's interesting. What are the stories about?

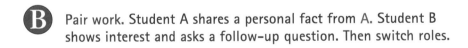

Useful Expressions:
Showing interest
Oh, really?
How interesting!
That's interesting.
That sounds interesting.
Me, too.
I know what you mean.

 C Pair work. Change partners three more times and share personal information.

D Choose the most interesting fact you heard. Report it to the class.

Used to

(A) Study the chart. Notice the different forms of *used to*.

> We use *used to* to talk about situations that were true or happened regularly in the past. These situations are not true now or do not happen anymore.
>
> A: I didn't use to know anything about computers.
> B: I know what you mean. I used to avoid them. Now I can't live without them.
>
> A: Did your father use to eat a lot of sugar?
> B: My father used to eat anything. Now he's more careful about his diet.

(B) Complete the sentences about *use(d) to*.

1. *Used to* is followed by _____.   **a.** the base form of a verb   **b.** a gerund (*-ing* form)

2. Use the base form *use to* in questions and _____ statements.   **a.** positive   **b.** negative

3. Use *used to* to talk about the _____.   **a.** present   **b.** past

(C) Each of the following sentences contains one mistake. Correct the mistakes.

1. I use to talk on the phone a lot.
2. Did you used to have long hair?
3. My computer never use to crash so often.
4. I didn't used to have a cell phone.
5. I use to borrow my friend's phone.
6. He never use to watch TV.

(D) Use the verbs in the box to describe each situation in Mary's life ten years ago and now. Use *used to* and the simple present.

> listen to   go to   wear
>
> watch   work on

1. Before: hip-hop music / Now: jazz
2. Before: jeans / Now: suit
3. Before: movie theater / Now: DVDs at home
4. Before: large PC / Now: small laptop computer

Mary used to listen to hip-hop music. Now she . . .

7 Communication

Your personal web page

People used to call him Tetsuya. Now everyone calls him ...

 Two years ago, Tetsuya and his family moved from Tokyo to Los Angeles. Look at his old Tokyo web page and his new Los Angeles web page. How has his life changed? Make sentences with *used to* and *didn't use to*.

Address: http://www.tokyohomepage.net/tetsuya.html ⟩ GO

- My name is Tetsuya.
- I live in Tokyo with my parents.
- I wear a uniform to school.
- I ride my bicycle to school.
- I belong to the soccer club.
- I study all the time, but my English isn't very good.

last updated: three years ago

Address: http://www.LAhomepage.net/tetsuya.html ⟩ GO

- Everyone here calls me "Ted." I like L.A. a lot.
- Guess what? I have a new niece! Her name is Risa.
- I don't wear a uniform.
- I have a car! I drive to college.
- I'm a member of my college's swim team.
- I have a lot of friends and we speak English together!

last updated: yesterday

 Make notes about your life five years ago and now. Try to write down things that are different if possible.

Five years ago	**Now**
Home: _____	Home: _____
Family: _____	Family: _____
Friends: _____	Friends: _____
Work/School: _____	Work/School: _____
Favorites (movies, magazines,	Favorites (movies, magazines,
TV programs): _____	TV programs): _____
Other: _____	Other: _____

C Pair work. Tell your partner how your life has changed in the past five years.

I used to live with my family at home but now I have my own apartment.

Technology Today

Lesson B | New ideas

1 Vocabulary Link

Describing products

A Look at these products. Read the description of each product.

1. It's durable. You won't have to buy a new one soon. It's portable. You can use it at home, the office, and on trips. It comes with a rechargeable battery.

2. You can trust this camera. It's very reliable. Because it's disposable, it's convenient. Use it once and then throw it away. Best of all, it's affordable. You can buy more than one without spending a lot of money.

3. This robot asks questions and sings songs. Your child will love to play with this interactive toy. There is nothing else like it on the market—it's very innovative. It's also cute, and very attractive.

B Match the definitions with the words in blue in A. Write the words below.

1. laptop computer
   a. can be used again ___rechargeable___
   b. easy to carry or move _____
   c. strong _____

2. underwater camera
   a. is thrown away after use _____
   b. inexpensive _____
   c. always works well _____

3. robot toy for children
   a. actively communicates _____
   b. nice to look at _____
   c. new and different _____

C Pair work. Think of a product. Use words from above to describe the product to your partner. Your partner guesses what the product is.

This product is like a portable office. I can use e-mail anywhere.

Is it a handheld computer?

2 Listening

Hi-tech toys

  A Listen to these two conversations.
Circle the best answer to complete each sentence. (CD 2, Track 36)

1. Lynn's best friend / pet / maid is a robot.

2. A lot of people in Finland play games on their computers / cell phones / televisions.

  B Listen again. For each conversation, circle the words the people use to describe the new technology. (CD 2, Track 37)

1. Conversation 1: **a.** not very affordable   **b.** happy   **c.** interactive

   d. rechargeable (batteries)   **e.** strange

2. Conversation 2: **a.** fun   **b.** innovative   **c.** old-fashioned   **d.** popular

3 Reading

Rescue robots

> Do you think robots are useful? Why or why not?

 A Read the title of the newspaper article on page 121. Then look at the photos and read the captions. What do you think this article is about?

_____

_____

_____

B Read the article. Number the steps (1 to 7) in the order that they happened.

a. _____ The roof of the gymnasium collapsed.

b. _____ Morgan was rescued.

c. _____ Morgan could not escape.

d. _____ Morgan went into the gymnasium.

e. _____ The robot located Morgan's position.

f. _____ Morgan was taken to the hospital.

g. _1_ There was a heavy snowfall.

World Link

"Paro" is a Japanese robotic toy used in hospitals and nursing homes. This seal-shaped robot acts like a real pet and is thought to reduce stress in patients.

The Fairview Herald

Local Girl Rescued

She may have a broken leg, but she can't be happier. Morgan Bailey, 11, is happy to be alive.

Tuesday was like any other day for Morgan. She was at school. It was fourth period, and she was the first student to arrive in the gymnasium for her physical education class.

Suddenly there was a loud noise.

"There was a sharp cracking noise and then a loud boom. After that, I don't remember anything," said Morgan.

The roof of the gymnasium had collapsed under the heavy snow. Morgan was trapped underneath. She couldn't escape.

"I woke up and there was a big piece of wood on my leg. I couldn't move it. I was starting to get cold."

Fortunately, help was nearby. A new program using "rescue robots" was tried for the first time.

"We were nervous about using the robot," said Derrick Sneed, the man in charge of the program. "But in the end, the robot gave us reliable information. It went extremely well."

The rescue robot was able to go into the gym and locate Morgan's exact position.

"We send in robots first because it may not be safe for humans," said Mr. Sneed. "Human beings are not as useful as robots in some situations. A gas leak, for example, could kill you or me but wouldn't hurt a robot."

Although it didn't happen in Morgan's case, some rescue robots can bring fresh air or water to people who are trapped.

Rescue robots go into rough, dangerous places. They work in life or death situations. They have to be durable.

Doctors say that Morgan is doing well. She should be going home in two or three days. What is the first thing she wants to do after she gets out of the hospital?

"I want to meet my hero," laughs Morgan. "That little robot that saved my life!"

A dangerous mess

ask**&**
ANSWER

Can you think of any other advantages to using rescue robots? In what other kinds of situations could rescue robots be used?

As...as

A Look at the pictures and read the sentences. Then answer the questions.

the Ariane rocket   the Boeing 747   the Airbus A330

The Ariane rocket is faster than the Boeing 747 and the Airbus A330.
The Boeing 747 and the Airbus A330 are not as fast as the Ariane rocket.
The Boeing 747 is as fast as the Airbus A330.

1. Which of the vehicles (pictured above) fly at the same speed?
   Which highlighted expression is used to show that?
2. Which highlighted expression shows that the Airbus 8330 and
   the Boeing 747 fly more slowly than the Ariane rocket?

B The digital pen is a new product that has a camera in it. Look at the comparison chart.
Use the words in parentheses to begin sentences using *as...as.*

	ballpoint	digital			ballpoint	digital
1. expensive	☐	✓	4. work well	✓	☐
2. write smoothly	☐	✓	5. durable	✓	✓
3. reliable	✓	✓	6. popular	✓	☐

1. (ballpoint pen) <u>The ballpoint pen isn't as expensive as the digital pen.</u>
2. (ballpoint pen) _____
3. (ballpoint pen) _____
4. (digital pen) _____
5. (digital pen) _____
6. (digital pen) _____

5 Writing

Modern technology

A Write about a useful technology or product that you
use or someone you know uses. Explain the ways that it
helps make life better.

A Technology I Like

I used to buy videotapes of movies, but
now I buy DVDs. I like DVDs because they
are easy to use. It is easy to find your
favorite scenes and DVDs are also very
durable. They last longer than
videotapes. They are also...

B Pair work. Exchange papers with a partner. Tell your partner any other
ways that you think this technology or product can make life better.

6 Communication

The wave of the future

A Pair work. Read about these five new products. In your opinion, which products do the words in the box describe? Tell your partner.

affordable	disposable	portable	reliable
attractive	innovative	rechargeable	

Throw-away cell phone

You can buy this inexpensive cell phone and throw it away after you've used up the minutes.

Self-defense jacket

When a stranger grabs you from behind, he receives an electric shock from your jacket.

Wearable computer

You can wear this convenient computer anywhere.

Hybrid car

This car gets energy from the brakes to recharge the battery.

Fly-sized robot

Doctors hope to use this tiny robot for surgery on their patients.

B Group work. Discuss the following questions with your group.

- Who would use each product?
- Would you use it? Why or why not?
- What might be one problem for each new item of technology?
- Which products will be common in the near future?
- Would these products improve our lives? If so, how?

C Group work. Look at the products again. Agree on a product for each category. You can use each product more than once.

- the most fun
- the most practical
- the most dangerous
- a product that isn't good for the environment

 Check out the World Link video.

 Practice your English online at <u>worldlink.heinle.com.</u>

1 Vocabulary Link

Tasks before a trip

kennel = a place where pets stay when their owners leave town

 A Andrew and Becky are going on a trip. What will they do before they leave home?
Match 1–6 with a–f. Then match 7–12 with g–l.

1. put	a. the trash	7. change	g. the house keys to a friend
2. unplug	b. the traveler's checks	8. give	h. the plants
3. empty	c. their pet in a kennel	9. stop	i. the lights
4. get	d. the bills	10. turn off	j. the voice mail message
5. give away	e. any electrical items	11. confirm	k. the mail delivery
6. pay	f. any fresh foods	12. water	l. the flight plans

B Look at the picture. Take turns telling what Andrew did and what Becky did.
Use the vocabulary in A.

C Think of a trip you've taken.
Which tasks did you do before you left home?

ask**&** ANSWER

What might happen if you forget to do some of the tasks in A?

2 Listening

While we're away, could you . . . ?

A Paula is asking Leticia for help. What does she ask Leticia to do? Check (✓) the task. (CD 2, Track 38)

☐ feed the dog   ☐ pick up the mail   ☐ water the plants

B Listen again. Write *P* for Paula or *L* for Leticia. (CD 2, Track 39)

1. __P__ is taking a trip for two weeks.
2. _____ is going to water the plants.
3. _____ is going to put the dog in the kennel.

4. _____ asked about the mail.
5. _____ stopped the mail delivery.
6. _____ will give the keys to _____.

ask & ANSWER

Do you ever ask your friends or neighbors for help? Why or why not?

World Link

The busiest air route in the world is between Hong Kong and Taipei. Every year, over four million passengers fly between the two cities.

Source: *Guinness World Records, 2004*

3 Pronunciation

Reduced *have to* and *has to*

A Listen to these sentences.
Notice the reduced pronunciation of *have to* and *has to*. (CD 2, Track 40)

1. I'm going to miss my flight. I have to hurry.
2. Everyone has to sit down before this plane can take off.

B Imagine that you and a friend are going on a trip to another country. How will you prepare? Make a list of tasks you and your friend have to do.

I have to . . .	My friend has to . . .

C Pair work. Now tell a partner about the tasks.

> I have to pack my suitcase.

> My friend has to get some traveler's checks.

4 Speaking

Have you finished packing?

A Mina and Esther are preparing to leave on a trip. Listen to their conversation. What is the problem? (CD 2, Track 41)

Esther: We have to leave in thirty minutes. Have you finished packing?

Mina: Yes, I have . . .

Esther: You look worried. What's wrong?

Mina: I can't remember where I put my passport.

Esther: Oh, no!

Mina: It's here somewhere.

Esther: When did you last have it?

Mina: About ten minutes ago. Let me think . . . Oh, there it is. I put it on the dresser.

Esther: What a relief!

B Pair work. Practice the conversation with a partner.

ask & _____
ANSWER
Talk about a time when you lost something. What did you do?

5 Speaking Strategy

Saying you've forgotten something

A Study the Useful Expressions in the chart. Practice saying the sentences.

Useful Expressions: Saying you've forgotten something	
I forgot + noun	I forgot my bus pass.
I forgot + infinitive	I forgot to empty the trash.
I don't remember + gerund	I don't remember turning off the lights.
I can't remember where + clause	I can't remember where I put my car keys.

B Pair work. You are going to perform a short conversation about forgetting something. Follow the steps below.

Step 1: Choose a location.

☐ the airport
☐ school
☐ the office

Step 2: Choose something you forgot to take or do.

☐ ticket
☐ report
☐ textbook

☐ get traveler's checks
☐ feed the dog
☐ other: _____

Step 3: Write and practice a short conversation with your partner. Then perform it for the class.

OK, it's time to get on the plane.   *Oh, no! I forgot my ticket.*

6 Language Link

Modal verbs of necessity

A We use *must, have to*, and *have got to* to express necessity. Study the chart below.

Modal verbs of necessity: *must, have to*, and *have got to*

	present forms	past forms
affirmative	I **must** confirm my flight. I **have** to confirm my flight. I **have got** to confirm my flight.	I **had** to confirm my flight.
negative	I **don't have** to confirm my flight.	I **didn't have** to confirm my flight.

B Read the sentences. Then circle all the answers that apply.

1. You can use ___ in the present form to express necessity.
     a. must   **b.** have to   **c.** have got to

2. Only the past form of ___ is used to express necessity.
     a. must   **b.** have to   **c.** have got to

3. You cannot use the negative form of ___ to express lack of necessity.
     a. must   **b.** have to

C These people are preparing for a trip. Look at their lists. They have finished the tasks that are checked (✓). On a separate piece of paper, write eight sentences with *has/have to* or *doesn't/don't have to*.

Jake

Jim and Doris

✓ *buy a backpack*
prepare a first aid kit
get shots
✓ *apply for a youth hostel card*

✓ **get traveler's checks**
✓ **pay the bills**
change the voice mail message
stop the mail delivery

D Correct the error in each sentence.

1. She doesn't has to pack her suitcase.

2. They must leave yesterday.

3. I haven't to reserve a hotel.

4. All passengers must to board the flight now.

5. We didn't had to pay in cash.

6. You don't have got to buy traveler's checks.

A Pair work. Imagine you are going on a camping trip. You will be in the forest, far away from any towns or cities. Follow these instructions:

- Circle the items that are necessary for your trip.
- Check (✓) the items that you would like to bring, but that are not necessary.
- Cross out the items that are not necessary.

sleeping bag

cell phone

flashlight

chewing gum

bottled water

canned food

back pack

Swiss army knife

first aid kit

money

lighter

thermos bottle

cooking pot

plastic plates and cups

tent

B Group work. Join another pair. Together you must decide what to take on your trip. You can only take six items. Choose four items pictured above, and decide on two that are not pictured. Think about:

- food
- shelter
- safety
- water
- first aid

We had better take the tent for shelter.

C Tell the class the items your group has decided to take and explain your reasons.

Let's Go Somewhere!

Lesson B | Adventures in traveling

1 Vocabulary Link 🔁

Airline travel

A Each word on the left matches with one on the right to form a compound noun about air travel. Write each compound noun below the picture it describes.

baggage	carry-on	flight	oxygen
boarding	check-in	overhead	tray

attendant	compartment	luggage	pass
claim	counter	mask	table

1. <u>tray</u>
    <u>table</u>

2. _____
    _____

3. _____
    _____

4. _____
    _____

5. _____
    _____

6. _____
    _____

7. _____
    _____

8. _____
    _____

B Use the compound words in A to complete the sentences below.

_____ **a.** When you arrive at the airport for your flight, you go to the <u>check-in counter</u> first.

_____ **b.** When your departing flight is announced, pick up your _____ _____ and go to the gate.

_____ **c.** Before you get on the plane, you must show your _____ _____ .

_____ **d.** When you enter the plane, you put your luggage in the _____ _____ .
You may need to ask a _____ _____ for help.

_____ **e.** Before takeoff, you learn about safety. They show you how to use an _____ _____
in an emergency.

_____ **f.** During the fight, you are served drinks on your _____ _____ .

_____ **g.** After the flight is over, you go to the _____ _____ area to get your luggage.

2 Listening

A long weekend

Many students and workers look forward to Monday or Friday holiday, because they can enjoy a "long weekend." What do you like to do on a long weekend?

A Listen. What did Jun do? Circle the correct answers. (CD 2, Track 42)

Jun flew / drove to three / four countries in three / four days.

B Listen again. Check (✓) the statements that are true for Jun. (CD 2, Track 43)

- [ ] 1. Jun loves flying.
- [ ] 2. Jun didn't go shopping.
- [ ] 3. Jun was in a hurry.
- [ ] 4. Jun had two pieces of luggage.
- [ ] 5. Jun didn't make a reservation.
- [ ] 6. Jun's flights were expensive.
- [ ] 7. Jun works for an airline.
- [ ] 8. Jun works in sales.

ask & ANSWER

Would you like to take a trip like Jun's? Why or why not? Where would you like to go on a long weekend?

World Link

Tired of economy class? By 2025, "scramjets" may be able to take passengers from New York to Tokyo in just one hour!

Source: *NASA*

3 Reading

Traveling alone

Would you like to take a vacation by yourself? Why or why not?

A Look at the article on page 131 and its title. What do you think the author is writing about? Check (✓) your answer. Then read the article and see if you were right.

- [ ] 1. the advantages of traveling alone
- [ ] 2. some memories of traveling alone
- [ ] 3. the expense of traveling alone

B Read the article again. What topics does the author mention about solo travel?

- [ ] 1. the cost of solo travel
- [ ] 2. the dangers of traveling alone
- [ ] 3. study vacations
- [ ] 4. using your vacation to learn a sport
- [ ] 5. packing for a trip alone
- [ ] 6. options for solo travelers

GOING SOLO IS THE WAY TO GO!

by D. Toor

How do you usually travel? Do you go with a close friend or a group of friends? Do you join a tour group? Do you travel with your family?

Have you ever imagined "going solo"? In the mid 1990s, it was estimated that 9 million Americans were planning a summer vacation alone. Since then, the number of solo travelers has increased.

You may think that traveling alone would be scary or boring. Well, according to people who do it, that's not exactly true. Solo travelers often have positive experiences: they make new friends, get to know themselves better, and can make their own schedules.

There are many different things you can do on a vacation alone. Some solo travelers use the time to learn or practice a sport such as golf, mountain climbing, or scuba diving. Others go and stay on a ranch and learn how to ride a horse. You can pretend to be a cowboy or a cowgirl for a day!

You may not believe this, but some travelers like to study on their vacation. They even go to "vacation college" at a university or join a research team as a volunteer worker. It's hard but satisfying work. You can "play scientist" for a week or two while you help someone with their project.

For solo travelers of different ages and genders, there are many travel options. There are tours for women only and for people over the age of 60. And, of course, there are trips for singles who are looking for romance. One company offers trips that focus on fine dining—there is time for sightseeing during the day and for sharing a delicious meal with new friends at night.

The next time you take a trip somewhere, why don't you consider going solo?

Bon voyage!

C Look at the items you checked in B. For each item, give examples from the reading.

1. _____

2. _____

3. _____

ask & ANSWER

What would you do on a vacation by yourself? What cities do you think are good destinations if you're traveling solo? Why do you think so?

The present perfect for indefinite time

A Study the chart. Notice how the present perfect is used in the conversations.

The present perfect is used for talking about past experiences viewed from the present. It is also used for talking about recently completed activities.		
A: **Have** you (ever) **been** to Bhutan? B: No, I haven't. Have you? A: Yes, I have. It's a really interesting country.	A: Let's see a movie. How about *Star Wars*? B: I've (already) **seen** it. A: Did you like it?	A: I've just **packed** the suitcases B: **Have** you **fed** the cats? A: No, not yet. I'll do that now.

B Look at the conversations below. Then read each statement. Write *T* for true, *F* for false, or *N* for not enough information.

1. Man: Do you want a sandwich?
   Woman: No, thanks. I've just finished lunch.
   • The woman ate lunch four hours ago. _____

2. Woman: Have you ever visited Rio?
   Man: Yes, I have.
   • The man went to Rio last year. _____

3. Man: Should I call a cab for you?
   Woman: No, Fred has already called one.
   • A cab was called. _____

4. Woman: What does Maria want?
   Man: I don't know, but she's called three times.
   • Maria just called. _____

5. Man: Have you been to London?
   Woman: I've been to England, but I've never been to London.
   • The woman just came back from London. _____

6. Woman: Have you already put the suitcases in the car?
   Man: Not yet. Can you do it?
   • The man has just moved the suitcases. _____

5 Writing

Travel experiences

A Write about places you have and haven't visited.

> I've been to Barcelona. It's a great city. I stayed there for almost two weeks. I visited the famous sites, such as La Rambla and . . .
> I haven't been anywhere in South America yet, but I am planning to go. Next year I will join a tour group. We will visit four countries, including . . .

B Pair work. Share your writing with a partner. Ask a question about the place your partner visited.

6 Communication

Find someone who has . . .

 Class activity. Follow these instructions.

1. Ask your classmates questions with the present perfect.
   Complete as much of the chart as you can.

2. When someone answers "Yes" to a question, ask another question to get more information.
   Then write the person's name and the piece of information in the chart.

> Jin Sung, have you ever visited a big city?

> What city have you visited?

> Yes, I have.

> Seoul, Korea.

Find someone who has . . .

1 visited a big city
2 joined a group tour
3 talked to a flight attendant
4 ridden on a train
5 gone on a trip and forgotten something
6 spent time on a beach
7 participated in a festival
8 seen a TV show about a foreign place
9 eaten food from another country
10 overpacked for a trip
11 gone on a day trip
12 taken a lot of photos of something

Name	Information

 Class activity. Get to know your classmates.
Listen to your teacher read each item in A.
If you've ever done the activity, raise your hand.

 Check out the World Link video.   **Practice your English online at** worldlink.heinle.com.

REVIEW: Units 10-12

1 Storyboard

A Pia is calling Bob at work. Complete the conversation. For some blanks, more than one answer is possible.

① Hello?

Hello. May I _____ Bob, please?

② _____ for a minute?

Sure.

③ I'm sorry, but _____. _____ leave a message?

④ Sure. Tell him _____.

Pia? _____ do you _____ that?

⑤ It's P as in _____, I _____, and A _____.

OK. I'll give him _____.

⑥ Hi, Bob. I'm skiing!

Pia? _____ are you?

B Group work. In groups of three, practice the conversation. Then change roles and practice again.

C Group work. Role play. Think of an interesting place to make a telephone call from. Then make your own conversation like the one above. Practice with your group.

A Pair work. Look at the picture of Mickey's house. How many items in the picture can you name? Take turns naming items.

B Pair work. Look at the picture again. Mickey went on a trip, but he forgot to do many things before he left. On a piece of paper, write down the items he forgot and the tasks he forgot to do.

C Pair work. Role play. Pretend you are Mickey and call a friend for help. Choose three things you forgot and ask for help. Then switch roles.

I don't remember turning out the light in the living room. Can you do it for me?

Sure. No problem.

3 Wide-screen TV

A Look at this ad for a wide-screen TV.
Circle the correct verb forms and unscramble the adjectives.

This Week's Best Buy!

Are you planning *(buying / to buy)* a new TV?
Do you want *(seeing / to see)* events as they really happen?
Can't stand *(viewing / to view)* movies at the wrong size?

Try our new wide-screen TV!

★ *it has an amazing sound system with large speakers.*

★ *It's _____ (attavicter).*

★ *The slim four-inch screen is _____ (venivation).*

★ *It's _____ (bialeler). Enjoy worry-free viewing.*

At $3,999, it may not seem _____ (fordaflabe).
Don't worry! We have a special payment plan.
Check out our wide-screen TV. You'll appreciate *(watching / to watch)* TV in a whole new way!

B Pair work. Compare your own TV to the one in A. Use comparatives and sentences with *(not) as . . . as.*

My TV is not as expensive as the wide-screen TV.

4 Old favorites

A Complete the chart with your favorites.

	When you were younger	Now
Snack food		
Music group or singer		
Piece of clothing you own(ed)		
Book or magazine		
TV show		
Color		

B Group work. Ask and answer questions about your present and past favorites.
Use *used to* for the past favorites. Have you changed a lot?

What snack food did you use to eat?

I used to eat pudding after school. I loved it!

5 First trip

A Emma Goldstein is ninety years old. She took her first trip on an airplane last month. Read what she said. Then correct the mistake in each sentence. It can be a mistake in grammar or vocabulary.

1. I used to ~~was~~ be afraid of flying.

2. Last month, I made a call from my daughter.

3. She said, "You must to pack your bags. We're taking a trip."

4. I didn't want to going, but I had no choice.

5. I took two pieces of boarding passes on the plane.

6. The flight attendant was nice. She helped me put everything in the oxygen mask.

7. Airplane travel is not as scarier as I thought.

8. I can now proudly say, "I have flying on an airplane!"

B Pair work. Ask your partner about a trip he or she has taken.

6 Listening: Could I speak to . . . ?

 Listen. Circle the correct answer for each question. (CD 2, Track 44)

1. What message did Sheila leave for Tom?

WHILE YOU WERE OUT	WHILE YOU WERE OUT	WHILE YOU WERE OUT
Sheila called. She wants to meet soon. She will call again at 5:00.	Sheila called. She can't meet tomorrow. Please call her.	Sheila called. She can't meet today. She wants to meet tomorrow at 2:00.

2. What message did Ted leave for Scott?

WHILE YOU WERE OUT	WHILE YOU WERE OUT	WHILE YOU WERE OUT
Ted called. His computer crashed. He wants you to fix it.	Ted called. He has a question about his new portable computer. Please call him.	Ted called. He wants to buy a new portable computer. He will call you.

Language Summaries

Unit 1 *All About Me*

Lesson A

Vocabulary Link

acquaintance
best friend
boyfriend
colleague
dating
girlfriend
parent
related
supervisor

Language Link

The simple present vs.
the present continuous

Speaking Strategy

Useful Expressions:
Introducing someone to someone else

Informal introductions
Junko, this is Ricardo.
Junko, meet Ricardo.

Formal introductions
I'd like you to meet Tammy.
Let me introduce Tammy.

Lesson B

Vocabulary Link

birth certificate
diploma
driver's license
electronic organizer
passport
report card
resume
student ID card
yearbook

Language Link

Review of the simple past

Unit 2 *Let's Eat!*

Lesson A

Vocabulary Link

bland
buttery
crispy
crunchy
healthy
juicy
oily
salty
sour
spicy
sweet

Language Link

The comparative form of adjectives

Speaking Strategy

Useful Expressions:
Offering and suggesting

Why don't we go to the pizza shop on
  the corner?
How about the restaurant downtown?
How about having a picnic in the park?

Lesson B

Vocabulary Link

appetizer
dessert
doggie bag
drive-through window
entree
junk food
takeout

Language Link

The superlative form of adjectives

Unit 3 *Unsolved Mysteries*

Lesson A

Vocabulary Link

arrest a criminal
break a law
catch a criminal
commit a crime
have an alibi
make a confession
question a criminal
solve a crime

Language Link

Stative verbs

Speaking Strategy

**Useful Expressions:
Talking about possibility**

I bet (that) . . .
There's a good chance (that) . . .
It's likely (that) . . .
I doubt (that) . . .
It doesn't seem possible (that) . . .
It's unlikely (that) . . .

Lesson B

Vocabulary Link

evidence
hoax
legend
mystifying
puzzling
testimony
vanished
weird

Language Link

Adverbs of manner

Unit 4 *Today's Trends*

Lesson A

Vocabulary Link

15 / 70 / 100 percent
a majority of
doubled / tripled / quadrupled
twice / three times
one fifth / one half / two thirds

Language Link

Quantity expressions:

all (of)
most (of)
a lot (of)
some (of)
a couple (of)
none (of)

Speaking Strategy

**Useful Expressions:
Disagreeing**

I don't agree.
I don't think so.
I disagree.
I don't think that's true.

Not necessarily.

Lesson B

Vocabulary Link

follow
individual
innovative
look (*n.*)
makeover
old-fashioned
outstanding
stylish
tailor-made

Language Link

Giving advice with *could, should, ought to,* and *had better*

Language Summaries

Unit 5 *In the Neighborhood*

Lesson A

Vocabulary Link

cut out coupons
get a haircut
go grocery shopping
pick up the dry cleaning
go to a dentist appointment
leave the car at the garage
make a grocery list
pick up the kids from school
take the bus home
unload the groceries

Language Link

Polite requests with modal verbs
and *mind*

Speaking Strategy

Useful Expressions:
Getting a clerk's attention in a store

Excuse me. Do you work here?
Sorry to bother you, but I have a question.
Are you busy? I need some help.

Lesson B

Vocabulary Link

congestion
convenient
greenery
high-rise
litter
pedestrian
run-down
subway

Language Link

Imperatives

Unit 6 *Student Life*

Lesson A

Vocabulary Link

apply to
attend
be accepted to
competitive
grade
reject
research
scholarship
semester

Language Link

Plans and decisions with
be going to and *will*

Speaking Strategy

Useful Expressions:
Asking about meaning

Does . . . mean . . . ?
What do you mean by . . . ?
I don't understand.
What does . . . mean?

Lesson B

Vocabulary Link

Definite future time expressions:

tomorrow
the day after tomorrow
in a few days
next week
the week after next
next summer
next year

Indefinite future time expressions:

one of these days
someday
sometime
sooner or later
in the future

Language Link

Predictions with *be going to* and *will*

Unit 7 *Let's Celebrate!*

Lesson A

Vocabulary Link

baby shower
bachelor party
barbecue
block party
family reunion
housewarming party
slumber party
surprise party

Language Link

Inviting using infinitives and
the *-ing* form

Speaking Strategy

Useful Expressions:
Accepting and refusing invitations

Accepting invitations

Sure!
That sounds great!
I'd love to.

Refusing invitations
I'm sorry, but I can't.
Unfortunately, I can't.
I'd love to, but I'm busy.

Lesson B

Vocabulary Link

advice
celebrate
colorful
come alive
costume
float
parade
sightseer
well-known

Language Link

Time clauses with *before*, *after*,
and *when*

Unit 8 *Fables and Fairy Tales*

Lesson A

Vocabulary Link

ant
crow
fox
frog
grasshopper
hare
lion
mouse
tortoise

Language Link

The past continuous

Speaking Strategy

Useful Expressions:
Asking about movies

What's the movie about?
What's the setting for the movie?
Who's in the movie?
What happens in the movie?

Lesson B

Vocabulary Link

brave
compassionate
determined
disciplined
evil
generous
loyal
wise

Language Link

The past continuous vs. the
simple past

Language Summaries

Unit 9 *The World of Work*

Lesson A

Vocabulary Link

active
careful
careless
dependent
flexible
inactive
independent
inflexible
late
pleasant
punctual
unpleasant

Language Link

The present perfect: *for* and *since*

Speaking Strategy

**Useful Expressions:
Asking about ability**

Can you spell well?
Are you able to type?
Are you good at cooking?
Do you know how to drive?

Lesson B

Vocabulary Link

farmhand
fashion designer
film director
fitness instructor
flight attendant
police officer
taxi driver
tour guide

Language Link

Verb + infinitive

Unit 10 *Telecommunications*

Lesson A

Vocabulary Link

answering machine
area code
cell phone
cord
international call
local call
long-distance call
public (tele)phone
receiver
(tele)phone directory
(tele)phone number

Language Link

Modal expressions used on the
telephone

Speaking Strategy

**Useful Expressions:
Spelling names**

Asking about spelling
How do you spell that?
Could you spell that?

Spelling:
It's Y-U-K-A.
Sure. It's (spelled) Y-U-K-A. That's Y as in
  yellow . . .

Lesson B

Vocabulary Link

answer a phone
call a wrong number
dial a wrong number
enter a phone number
get a busy signal
hear a busy signal
hang up a phone
leave a message
make a phone call
pay a phone bill
pick up a receiver
receive a phone bill
receive a phone call
take a message
try a phone number

Language Link

Verb + gerund vs. verb + infinitive

Unit 11 *Technology Today*

Lesson A

Vocabulary Link

address
crash
hardware
icon
menu
mouse
surf
window

Language Link

Used to

Speaking Strategy

Useful Expressions:
Showing interest

Oh, really?
How interesting!
That's interesting.
That sounds interesting.
Me, too.
I know what you mean.

Lesson B

Vocabulary Link

affordable
attractive
disposable
durable
innovative
interactive
portable
rechargeable
reliable

Language Link

As . . . as

Unit 12 *Let's Go Somewhere!*

Lesson A

Vocabulary Link

change the voice mail message
confirm the flight plans
empty the trash
get the traveler's checks
give away any fresh foods
give the house keys to a friend
pay the bills
put your pet in a kennel
stop the mail delivery
turn off the lights
unplug any electrical items
water the plants

Language Link

Modal verbs of necessity

Speaking Strategy

Useful Expressions:
Saying you've forgotten something

I forgot + **noun:**
I forgot my bus pass.

I forgot + **infinitive:**
I forgot to empty the trash.

I don't remember + **gerund:**
I don't remember turning off the lights.

I can't remember **where** + **clause:**
I can't remember where I put my car keys.

Lesson B

Vocabulary link

baggage claim
boarding pass
carry-on luggage
check-in counter
flight attendant
overhead compartment
oxygen mask
tray table

Language Link

The present perfect for indefinite time

Grammar Notes

Lesson A

Language Link: The simple present vs. the present continuous

Use the simple present to talk about habits, routines, schedules, and general truths:

> I always **take** a shower in the morning.
> The express train **arrives** at 9:03 a.m.
> They are from Switzerland. They **don't speak** German. They **speak** French.
> Hot air **rises.**

Use the simple present to talk about situations of long duration:

> I **live** at 516 Elm Street.

Use the present continuous to talk about actions that are happening at the time of speaking:

> She**'s talking** on the phone and the baby **is crying.**
> Look at that car! It**'s speeding!**

Use the present continuous to talk about temporary situations:

> We**'re living** in San Diego for the summer.

Use the present continuous to talk about actions happening *in the extended present,* but not at the *exact* moment of speaking:

> I**'m not sleeping** well this week.

Lesson B

Language Link: Review of the simple past

Use the simple past to talk about actions that started and ended in the past:

> I **started** college in 1998. I **graduated** in 2002.

The actions can be long or short in duration:

> He **dropped** the glass, but it **didn't break.**
> I **lived** in the same apartment for five years.

The past tense ending of regular verbs is *–ed*. Many verbs have irregular past tense endings:

Regular Past Tense Verbs				Irregular Past Tense Verbs			
change	changed	paint	painted	be	was/were	know	knew
check	checked	play	played	choose	chose	make	made
complete	completed	practice	practiced	come	came	meet	met
die	died	print	printed	do	did	read	read
finish	finished	receive	received	eat	ate	run	ran
graduate	graduated	sign	signed	forget	forgot	sleep	slept
help	helped	study	studied	give	gave	sing	sang
live	lived	talk	talked	get	got	take	took
lock	locked	travel	traveled	go	went	think	thought
marry	married	use	used	have	had	win	won
move	moved	work	worked	keep	kept	write	wrote

Lesson A

Language Link: The comparative form of adjectives

The Comparative Form of Adjectives

One syllable		Two syllables		Three syllables	
sweet	sweet**er**	simple	simpl**er**	relaxing	**more** relaxing
large	larg**er**	spicy	spic**ier**	delicious	**more** delicious
big	big**ger**	crowded	**more** crowded	interesting	**more** interesting
		famous	**more** famous		

One-syllable adjectives: Add –*er*. Add –*r* if the adjective ends in *e*. Double the final consonant and add –*er* if the adjective ends in a single vowel and a consonant.

Two-syllable adjectives: Some common two-syllable adjectives ending in an unstressed syllable (such as *simple, clever,* or *quiet*) form the comparative with -*er* or -*r*. Change final -*y* to -*ies*. Other adjectives, particularly those ending in -*ing, -ed, -ious,* or -*ful,* form the comparative with *more.*

Adjectives of three or more syllables: Add *more.*

The comparative form of *good* is *better.* The comparative form of *bad* is *worse.*

Use the comparative form of an adjective to compare two things:

I am tall, but Stan is **taller.**

This restaurant is **bigger than** that one. Your entree is **more expensive than** mine.

Sometimes you can use the comparative without *than:*

I am tall, but Stan is **taller.**

Lesson B

Language Link: The superlative form of adjectives

The Superlative Form of Adjectives

One syllable		Two syllables		Three syllables	
sweet	**the** sweet**est**	simple	**the** simpl**est**	relaxing	**the most** relaxing
large	**the** larg**est**	spicy	**the** spic**iest**	delicious	**the most** delicious
big	**the** big**gest**	crowded	**the most** crowded	interesting	**the most** interesting
		famous	**the most** famous		

One-syllable adjectives: Add *the* and –*est* or -*st.*

Two-syllable adjectives: Some common two-syllable adjectives ending in an unstressed syllable (such as *simple, clever,* or *quiet*) form the superlative with the and -*est* or -*st.* (Change the final -*y* to -*iest.*) Other adjectives, particularly those ending in -*ing, -ed, -ious,* or -*ful,* form the superlative with *the most.*

Adjectives of three or more syllables: Add *the most.* The superlative form of *good* is *the best.*

The superlative form of *bad* is *the worst.*

Use the superlative form of an adjective to compare something to an entire group:

Mimi is **the quietest** girl at school. Mud pie is **the most delicious** dessert of all.

You can use prepositional phrases after the superlative:

> Mount Everest **is the highest** mountain *in the world.*

You can use *one of* before the superlative to show that something or someone is part of a group:

> Jim, Kim, and Amy scored 100% on the test. Amy is **one of** the **best** students in our class.

Unit 3 *Unsolved Mysteries*

Lesson A

Language Link: Stative verbs

Thinking verbs	Having verbs	Feeling verbs	Sensing verbs	Other verbs	
believe	belong	appreciate	feel *	appear *	prefer
forget	have *	dislike	hear	be	seem
know	own	hate	see *	cost	want
remember	possess	like	smell *	look *	
think *		love	sound	mean	
understand			taste *	need	

Stative verbs describe states rather than actions. They are not usually used in continuous tenses:

> I prefer tea to coffee. Incorrect: ~~I am preferring tea to coffee.~~

Note: Certain stative verbs are also used in the continuous form. When used in this way, their meaning changes. These verbs are marked by an asterisk (*) in the chart above:

> He *looks* dangerous. (look = appear) He *is looking* at me. (look = watch)
> I *think* he is dangerous. (think = believe) I *am thinking* about the problem. (think = consider)
> She *saw* the crime. (see = look at) She *is seeing* the doctor tomorrow. (see = visit)

Lesson B

Language Link: Adverbs of manner

Use adverbs of manner to tell *how* something is done. They often end in *–ly:*

> I always eat lunch **quickly.**
> Study the problem **carefully.** Then mark your answer.

Some common adverbs of manner don't end in *–ly*. Some examples are: *fast, slow, hard,* and *late:*

> She drives too **fast.**
> He often works **late.**

Well is an irregular adverb. Its adjective form is *good:*

> Fluffy is a *good* dog. You trained her *well.*

Unit 4 *Today's Trends*

Lesson A

Language Link: Quantity expressions

Quantity expressions are used to talk about amounts.
All of these quantity expressions, except *a couple of*, can be used with both count and noncount nouns.

With count nouns	
All of Most of A lot of Some of A couple of None of	my friends follow trends.

With noncount nouns	
All of Most of A lot of Some of ---- None of	my homework is finished.

Lesson B

Language Link: Giving advice with *could, should, ought to,* and *had better.*

Use *should* or *ought to* to give advice:

    You **should** get a makeover.   You **ought to** get a makeover.

It is more common to use the negative form of *should* than the negative form of *ought to:*

    You **shouldn't** go there. It's too expensive.

Use *could* or *might* to make a suggestion. They are weaker than *should* or *ought to.* Do not use the negative form of *could* or *might* to make a suggestion:

    You **could** wear your new dress to the party.

    You couldn't wear your new dress to the party. } These are not suggestions.
    You might not wear your new dress to the party.

Could is often used when there is more than one choice.

    You **could** wear this dress or that one.

Use *had better (not)* to give strong advice. It sometimes sounds like a warning:

    You **had better wear** a suit. It's a formal occasion.   You **had better not** leave too late. You'll miss your flight.

Unit 5 *In the Neighborhood*

Lesson A

Language Link: Polite requests with modal verbs and *mind*

You can use *could you, would you, can you,* and *will you* to ask for a favor:

    A: Could/Would/Can you please answer the door?
    B: Sure.

Can you is usually used for more informal requests:

>A: **Can you** help me with my homework?
>B: No problem.

You can also use *would you mind* + the *–ing* form of the verb to make a request:

>A: **Would you mind** <u>picking up</u> the dry cleaning?
>B: No, not at all.

Lesson B

Language Link: Imperatives

The imperative form is the base form of the verb. Use imperatives to give commands, directions, or instructions, warnings, and advice:

>Jimmy! **Come in** here and **clean** your room!
>**Go** straight for two blocks. **Turn** left at the drugstore.

>**Add** two eggs and sugar. Then **stir** it.
>**Try** this medicine. It really works.

Use *don't* before the base form to make the negative imperative:

>**Don't cross** the street yet.

Add *please* to an imperative to make it more polite:

>*Please* **step** back! It's dangerous.

Unit 6 *Student Life*

Lesson A

Language Link: Plans and decisions with *be going to* and *will*

Be going to is always followed by the base form of the verb:

>I am **going to** *study* economics.   He **is going to** *live* in the dormitory.

Use *be going to* to talk about future plans. It is used for plans you made in the past. Do not use *will* in these situations:

>I applied to college. I was accepted. **I'm going to** attend Harvard University in the fall.

Form *yes/no* questions with *be going to* like this: *be* + subject + *going to* + base form of verb:

>**Are** you **going to** attend Harvard University?

Form *wh-* questions like this: *wh-* word + *be going to* + base form of verb:

>**When are** you **going to** start school?

Use future time expressions like *tomorrow, in a few days, next week,* and *next year* in sentences with *be going to:*

>She**'s going to** visit the campus *next week.*

Will is always followed by the base form of the verb:

>You**'ll** receive a paycheck soon.

Use both *be going to* and *will* to talk about general truths in the future:

>The new students **will** arrive on September 2. The new students **are going to** arrive on September 2.

Use *will* to make a sudden decision. (Do not use *be going to* in these situations.):

>There are no more seats on this train. We**'ll** take the bus, then.

Lesson B

Language Link: Predictions with *be going to* and *will*

Use both *be going to* and *will to* make general predictions about the future:
> In five years, I'll be the head of this department.
> He's going to do something interesting with his life.

With predictions, words like *probably* and *maybe* are often used:
> We'll *probably* move in a year or two.
> *Maybe* they'll get married.

Use *be going to*, but not *will*, when you have proof that something is going to happen:
> Watch out! That rock is going to fall!
> She's going to have a baby.

Unit 7 *Let's Celebrate!*

Lesson A

Language Link: Inviting using infinitives and the *-ing* form

Use *Do you want . . .* , *Would you like . . .* , or *How would you like . . .* with the infinite form of verb to extend an invitation:
> Do you want *to see* a movie?
> Would you like *to come* to my party?
> How would you like *to join* me for dinner tonight?

You can also use *Would you be interested in . . .* with the -ing form of the verb to extend an invitation:
> Would you be interested in *seeing* a movie?

Lesson B

Language Link: Time clauses with *before, after,* and *when*

Time clauses are formed with time words like *before, after,* and *when.* In formal written English, a time clause usually doesn't stand alone. It is connected to a main clause:

> [time clause]   [main clause]
> When I told him the message, he looked upset.

Use *before* in a time clause to show that the event in the main clause happened at an earlier time:
> Before I left home, I kissed the kids goodbye. (first = kissed kids; second = left home)

Use *after* in a time clause to show that the event in the main clause happened at a later time:
> After he sang Christmas carols, he went to bed. (first = sang; second = went to bed)

Use *when* in a time clause to show that the events happened at the same time or one immediately after the other:
> When you see a friend, you say "hello."

Time clauses can come before or after the main clause. Notice the use of the comma:
> After they arrive home, they eat special rice cakes.
> They eat special rice cakes after they arrive home.

Unit 8 *Fables and Fairy Tales*

Lesson A

Language Link: The past continuous

Use the past continuous for actions *in progress* in the past. It may not be clear if the action was completed or not:

> Last year, I **was studying** in college.

The action may be temporary:

> I **was leaving** home. Suddenly, there was a loud noise. I went back inside to see.

You can use the past continuous to show gradual change:

> The noise **was getting** louder and louder.

We don't usually use stative verbs (e.g., *be, want, like, feel*) in continuous tenses.

Lesson B

Language Link: The past continuous vs. the simple past

Use the past continuous to express an action *in progress*. Use the simple past to express a *completed* action:

> She **was getting into** the taxi.   She **got into** her car and **drove** away.

When there are two actions, the longer action is usually in the past continuous. It is interrupted by the shorter action in the simple past:

> I **was taking** a shower when the telephone **rang.**

The past continuous can show a temporary situation. The simple past shows a more permanent situation:

> Tom **was working** this morning.   Tom **worked** as a translator before he became a teacher.

Use the past continuous to introduce background information. Use the simple past to describe what happened next:

> The sun **was shining** and the birds **were singing.** Suddenly, someone **screamed.**

Unit 9 *The World of Work*

Lesson A

Language Link: The present perfect; *for* and *since*

Form the present perfect with the auxiliary *have* + past participle. For most verbs, the past participle is the same as the simple past form. However, there are many verbs that have irregular past participles:

Regular verbs			Irregular verbs		
Present	Past	Past Participle	Present	Past	Past Participle
fix	fixed	fixed	be	was/were	been
hum	hummed	hummed	come	came	come
live	lived	lived	drink	drank	drunk
study	studied	studied	get	got	gotten
talk	talked	talked	go	went	gone
walk	walked	walked	have	had	had

Use the present perfect for actions that started in the past and continue up until now. The actions may continue into the future as well:

I**'ve lived** here for two years. (I still live here.)

Use *for* and *since* with the present perfect. Use *for* + a period of time. Use *since* + a point in time or with a past time clause:

I**'ve lived** here *for* two years.
I**'ve lived** here *since* June 1st.
I**'ve lived** here *since* I was a child.

Lesson B

Language Link: Verb + infinitive

Certain verbs can be followed by the infinitive as an object. Some examples are: *agree, arrange, attempt, choose, decide, expect, forget, hate, hope, learn, like, love, need, plan, prepare, start, try,* and *want*:

I **like to sing.** I **want to become** a singer.

The main verb can be in different tenses.

I *decided* **to leave.** Their baby *is starting* **to speak.** You*'ll need* **to lift** heavy objects.

Unit 10 *Telecommunications*

Lesson A

Language Link: Modal expressions used on the telephone

Use *May I* or *Can I* to ask for permission:

May I speak to Thomas, please?   **Can I** leave a message?

Use *Can you* or *Could you* to make a polite request:

Could you hold for a minute, please?   **Can you** call back later?

Use *Would you like* to ask about preference:

Would you like to leave a message?

Lesson B

Language Link: Verb + gerund vs. verb + infinitive

Verbs followed by infinitive		Verbs followed by gerund		Verbs followed by infinitive or gerund	
agree	plan	appreciate	finish	begin	like
choose	prepare	avoid	hate	can't stand	love
decide	seem	can't help	imagine	continue	prefer
hope	want	dislike	keep	hate	try
learn	would like	enjoy	(not) mind		
need		feel like	suggest		

Unit 11 *Technology Today*

Lesson A

Language Link: *Used to*

Used to is followed by the base form of the verb:
> I **used to** *live* on Monroe Street.

Used to is a special past tense form. Use it to talk about things that were true or happened regularly in the past, but are not true or do not happen in the present:
> I always **used to** eat dessert with my dinner.
> People **used to** send letters through the post office. Now many people communicate by e-mail.

Questions and negatives are usually formed with *did (not) + use to*. Notice the spelling *(use to)*:
> We **didn't use to** have a laptop computer.
> **Did** you **use to** work for a large trading company?

Lesson B

Language Link: *As . . . as*

Use *as . . . as* to show that two things are equal:
> The Boeing 747 is **as fast as** the Airbus 8330.

Use *not as . . . as* to show that they are not equal:
> My computer is**n't as fast as** your computer.

After *as . . . as*, you can use a subject pronoun + a verb. In informal, spoken English you can use an object pronoun:
> She is **as strong as** *he is*.   She is **as strong as** *him*. (spoken/informal)
> She works **as efficiently as** he does.

These two sentences have the same meaning:
> The 747 is**n't as fast as** the Ariane Rocket. = The Ariane Rocket is faster than the 747.

Unit 12 *Let's Go Somewhere!*

Lesson A

Language Link: Modal verbs of necessity

Must is used to show necessity or obligation with reference to the present and future:

> I **must** go the airport immediately.   I **must** go to the airport tomorrow morning.

Must is often used in formal or official situations. It is also common in written rules or instructions. Sentences using *you + must* often imply a sense of authority on the part of the speaker:

> You **must** show your ID card to enter the building.

Have to is the most commonly used expression of necessity because it can be used with all tenses. The negative form of *have to* means "is not necessary":

> She **has to** go to the airport, but she **doesn't have to** check any luggage.
> We **had to** wait in line at the airport for two hours.

Like *must, have got to* is used to show necessity or obligation with reference to the present and future. It is used in spoken English and is less formal:

> Stop playing video games all the time! You**'ve got to** study more!

Lesson B

Language Link: The present perfect for indefinite time

Use the present perfect for past actions when the time they happened is unknown or unimportant. You cannot use the present perfect if you mention a specific time. Use the simple past instead:

> I**'ve been** to Korea.

> *I went* to Korea *last year.*
> *I went* to Korea *when I was in high school.*

Never means "at no time in the past." *Ever* means "at any time in the past up until now." It is used in questions with the present perfect:

> I**'ve been** to Brazil, but I**'ve** *never* **visited** Rio.   **Have** you *ever* **visited** Rio de Janeiro?

You can also use the present perfect for repeated actions in the past:

> I**'ve taken** this driving test three times.

Use the adverbs *already* or *yet* to talk about whether an action has been completed or not.
Use *already* with affirmative sentences and questions (especially when you are surprised that someone has done something). Notice its position in the sentence:

> I**'ve** *already* **packed** my suitcase.   **Have** you **packed** your suitcase *already?* That was fast!
> I**'ve packed** my suitcase *already.*   **Have** you *already* **packed** your suitcase?

Use *yet* with negative statements and questions. Notice its position in the sentence:

> **Have** you **applied** for your passport *yet?*   I **haven't applied** for my passport *yet.*

Answers

page 113, 6. Communication, Activity A

Answers: **1.** b, **2.** a, **3.** c, **4.** b